COLORADO
BOULDERING 2

BENNINGFIELD & SAMET

Colorado Bouldering

by Phillip Benningfield and Matt Samet

Front cover photo of Elizabeth Culbertson at Green Mountain by Fred Knapp.

ISBN# 1-892540-26-6

For a complete list of titles available from Sharp End Publishing, write to P.O. Box 1613, Boulder, CO 80306 or contact us through our website *www.sharpendbooks.com*. Sharp End Publishing is constantly seeking new material. Queries for climbing and outdoor guides are always welcome.

READ THIS BEFORE USING THIS GUIDE BOOK

Rock climbing, including bouldering, is extremely dangerous. A small and incomplete list of possible dangers include: loose rock, bad landings (eg. landing on uneven or rocky terrain, landing on a spotter). Unlike roped climbing, every bouldering fall is a ground fall. As a result, the boulderer risks serious injury or death with every attempt. Falls are common while bouldering.

The symbols used in this guide describe boulders with almost certain injury potential. It is, however, highly probable that you could seriously injure yourself on a problem that doesn't receive a highball or bad landing designation.

THE AUTHORS AND PUBLISHER EXPRESSLY DISCLAIM ALL REPRESENTA- TIONS AND WARRANTIES REGARDING THIS GUIDE, THE ACCURACY OF THE INFORMATION CONTAINED HEREIN, AND THE RESULTS OF YOUR USE HEREOF, INCLUDING WITHOUT LIMITATION, IMPLIED WARRANTIES OF MERCHANTABILITY AND FITNESS FOR A PARTICULAR PURPOSE. THE USER ASSUMES ALL RISK ASSOCIATED WITH THE USE OF THIS GUIDE.

It is your responsibility to take care of yourself while bouldering. Seek a professional instructor or guide if you are unsure of your ability to handle any circumstances that may arise. This guide is not intended as an instructional manual.

INTRODUCTION

Unlike roped climbing, bouldering relies on mental and physical dynamism, not the mastery of equipment. Bouldering is fun, allowing you to expend your precious climbing energy on movement and laughter rather than fiddling metal widgets into some jingus, flaring fist crack. A boulderer's frugal needs allow more time for actual climbing.

Bouldering has gone BIG in the last five years, a far cry from the more complacent early days of the sport when only esoteric oddballs and climbers training for bigger rocks took to the boulderfields. It has metamorphosed from an excuse to get a great workout to a hip pursuit unto itself, with hordes of newly-addicted climbers heading out bouldering for the sake of bouldering itself. Aided by ever-more springy crash pads, today's boulderers seek out and climb lines that were once considered too dangerous or difficult. This "keen new" eye has opened up an array of areas and problems that were previously ignored, providing a host of exceptional new problems for diehards and dilettantes alike.

Since the Founding Fathers of Front Range bouldering have already picked all the plums near the road, this batch of recent finds includes boulders far, far away from the hustle and bustle of civilization. Thusly, a broken ankle can spell the beginnings of a prolonged epic. Don't be fooled into thinking that these "new school" approaches will be short. Many of the areas covered in this book require up to an hour of (sometimes) grueling hiking. Other boulder fields have been highlighted with a few boulders to show the vast potential in overlooked or forgotten areas.

We conspired to include as many freshly developed areas as possible. Certain areas, even though they offer substantial numbers of boulder problems, have been excluded due to fragile ecosystems, touchy access issues or the wishes of concerned locals. Oh well. We can still play at the other areas so many boulderers were kind enough to share!

HISTORY

Because this guide focuses primarily on newly climbed rock, bouldering history is somewhat limited. Nevertheless, here is a quick glance at the latest boulderfields and the climbers who "discovered" them (of course, not every prolific individual can be included).

THE FRONT RANGE

The South Platte, probably the largest concentration of boulders in the state, has seen some recent development at sensitive areas with access issues, which are not included in this guide. At areas like Elevenmile Canyon, Sphinx Rock and Turkey Rocks, a number of fine problems have been established. It would be inconclusive to say these are first ascents as climbers have been on the rock for decades. Suffice it to say, many Colorado climbers like Steve Cheney, Mark Milligan, Bob Murray and Ian Spencer-Green have had occasion to put up dozens of stellar problems stretching up and down the Platte's expanse.

The exemplary Millennium Boulder and Ridgetop Boulders in Matthews-Winters Park were developed by Greg Johnson, Bob Williams, Mike Hickey and others in the late 90s as an alternative to the tired grease of nearby Morrison, which these talented locals had climbed out thousands of times over. With its close proximity to Denver and tall varnished faces, the Millennium Boulder continues to yield hard, stellar problems at the cutting edge of difficulty.

Introduction

The long-overlooked cache of giant boulders at mile marker 268 in Clear Creek Canyon first came to the notice of Denverite Greg Johnson in the summer of 2000. Realizing the enormity of his task, Johnson recruited the assistance of his brother Eric Johnson, Rufus Miller, Bob Williams, Mike Hickey and Matt Samet in whipping these water-polished, gneiss beasties into shape.

New activity in the Flatirons has taken place all over the map, encompassing newly-revisited areas from Green Mountain on the north all the way south to Eldorado Springs Canyon.

Eldorado Springs Canyon has seen a massive resurgence of activity, yielding new problems ranging from the conglomerate of the East Draw to new lines in Westworld to the more remote areas off the Eldorado Canyon Trail. Much of the development has been spearheaded by hyper-motivated Eldo locals Eric Johnson and Chip Ruckgaber, with other climbers like Mike Brooks, John Baldwin, Colin Lantz, John Dunne, Bart Streghe, Paul Lembeck, Scott Rennak and Matt Samet pitching in as well.

Another Horan find, the Upper Blues boulders above Big Bluestem Trail, saw further bouldering exploration during the spring of 2001, when Josh Deuto and Matt Samet filled in the blanks on the giant Mamoonious boulder and found a sweet stash of six solid, shady blocks only three minutes up the gully. Though remote, the area should continue to yield new problems in the years to come.

The Terrain Boulders, aka Droegerland, saw extensive activity by Jay Droeger, Miah Johnson, Tom Gage, Patrick Wilde and others during the 1998-1999 season. Though other climbers had visited this well-hidden cache of Fountain monsters over the years, most of their efforts went undocumented, and many of the best problems went overlooked.

The extensive and varied network of maroon and burgundy boulders on the back side of Green Mountain was secretly developed by Bob Horan during the 1990s. Drawn in by the allure of the various fall lines of sandstone blocks cascading off the west side of the Sacred Cliffs, Horan quietly established a host of great problems in this peaceful, immaculate setting.

The Upper Satellite boulders, a collection of scattered but aesthetic blocks in the serene valley between the 2nd and 3rd Flatirons was developed by various individuals, including Bart Streghe, John Dunne and Phillip Benningfield.

Gross Reservoir fell into disregard after Bob Horan et. al. developed a few blocks in the late 80's; during this time some mindless twit chipped many stellar lines, ruining entire blocks for future generations. A few worthy souls, Paul Lembeck, Colin Lantz, Jay Droeger, K. Rong and others who wish to remain anonymous rediscovered the cooler granite and developed scattered blocks on many of the hillsides. In the past two years the Damnation Boulders, The Burn and the Freight Train have seen concerted efforts and the known boulders have been filled in with problems up to V12 (a grade absent from Colorado since the Holloway era).

Aged bolts in a couple of rocks evidence Camp Dick's first forays, but the bouldering interest began with Colin Lantz. The area quickly fell into disfavor but Jay Droeger, John Dunn, the Hardman and many other Boulderites have rekindled recent interest. The Dick is now a destination spot for many Front Range boulderers during the hot summer months.

OTHER COLORADO AREAS

Monte Vista saw the influx of sport climbers many years ago, but not until the last two years did heavy-duty bouldering development occur. One of the original climbers to set his sights on the blocks was Josh Boe, who shared the find with Pat Wilde. Since then the effort has been shared by too many to mention.

Unaweep Canyon and Independence Pass see constant attention and new problems, some considered the best done to date, have been climbed by Chris Gopelrud, Matt L. and those who wish to remain anonymous.

Red Cliff sees yearly additions to the already developed blocks at the Kluttergarden in the form of ultra-thin crimpfests and tall, scary problems.

In the Penitente Canyon area a few discreet easy lines have been done near the Rock Garden with many more wating for the motivated boulderer.

ACCESS

Access is more and more a touchy subject in the climbing community. As our numbers swell, impact becomes more readily visible. Some areas were omitted from this guide either because they were partially on private land, or because locals politely asked us not to include them, or because climbing was already an endangered activity.

There are two immediate ways you can help with access issues: **Don't** trespass and **Do** join the Access Fund (www.accessfund.org). Remember, while out bouldering do your best to reduce impact on the land and other people's psyches. Be discreet with chalk, avoid using tick marks and don't project an overbearing verbal presence in areas with other users. In other words, use common sense. If you don't have any common sense then bring a friend who is more in touch with their humanity to help you out.

As of press time (Winter, 2002) Boulder Open Space and Mountain Parks was developing a new visitor plan that may or may not include closures, particularly on the west side of the Boulder Mountain Parks. If you would like to stay informed about access issues in the Flatirons, please send your name and e-mail address to the Flatirons Action Network at flatironsbouldering@yahoo.com. While FAN opposes any new closures, it is also committed to disseminating information about the Flatirons, organizing climbers on a grassroots level (whether politically or for clean-up days) and working with OSMP to keep areas open.

AREA/PROBLEM NAMES AND DESCRIPTIONS

This guide is loaded with a plethora of bouldering areas and names. Some names may have fallen into obscurity or disuse, requiring us to use a more contemporary, albeit dull name. If we inadvertently rename or re-rate an already-established problem, we apologize.
You may find some problem names to be offensive. In the interest of upholding the First Amendment we plead no contest. If a particularly offensive name raises your hackles, remember, the first ascentionist is probably at fault. Political correctness is not a bouldering technique, nor should it be. Better to just forget about it and move on to the next problem.

First Ascent Ethics

When it comes to bouldering, the rock is your friend. Would you poke, hit and prod at your friend with a sharp, metal object? The idea behind bouldering is to enjoy the rock on its own terms, appreciating it in its natural state. If you're fortunate enough to find a pristine boulder, take a moment to consider what the process of putting up new problems involves:

• It doesn't involve chipping or over-vigorous cleaning (i.e. Choss is choss so don't spend hours dicking away on some worthless pile that's best left alone in the first place).

• Cleaning a hold properly involves removing cobwebs and dirt but not solid rock. A toothbrush or wire brush should be sufficient.

• If you're an unfortunate witness to the sordid act of chipping or any other such bad behavior, speak up immediately! Better that we police ourselves before the land management authorities get involved.

• Lastly, the rock is not the only concern when developing an area—trees are our buddies as well and should not be cut down to make room for a problem. Too many limbs, bushes and full-grown trees have fallen by the wayside in the name of bouldering progress!

OSMP and Bouldering

Long before the bouldering explosion of the 1990s, the rock formations found on Open Space and Mountain Parks (OSMP) has attracted climbers from around the world. The diversity of outcroppings and boulderfields found here provides challenges for climbers of all abilities. With the increase in popularity of bouldering over the last few years, the impact on our fragile environment has been greatly magnified.

As a community, we are all responsible for ensuring the long-term integrity of our lands. As land managers, OSMP is entrusted with the protection of the natural resources of Open Space and Mountain Parks for this and future generations.

Many of the areas described in this book lie in the fragile and unique Boulder Mountain Parks, which is overseen by Boulder Open Space and Mountain Parks (OSMP). Bearing in mind that access and preservation are everyone's responsibility, we've collaborated with OSMP to bring you the OSMP rules and regulations regarding bouldering in the parks:

• Keep your crash pad off vegetation; only use pads in areas where vegetation is not present.

• Do not *garden, groom, scrub, clean, chip* or *glue* problems.

• Cutting vegetation, removing lichen or moss, gluing holds and altering resources is punishable by fines up to $1000.

• Leave your dog at home. All dogs must be on a hand-held leash on OSMP land unless under voice and sight control. This is extremely difficult while you are climbing unless someone specifically attends to the dog.

A BOULDERING ETHIC

• Leave the rocks and area surrounding them in a natural condition.

• Do not cut or remove plants, moss, or lichen, move rocks or glue holds.

• Stay on signed designated trails; use only designated areas where impact has already occurred.

• Never build your own trails, stairs or platforms.

• Avoid placing crash pads or gear on vegetation.

• Leave dogs at home.

• Be considerate of wildlife and other users. Respect all wildlife closures.

• Pack out all litter.

• Know and abide by all regulations.

• And most importantly, accept responsibility for yourself and others.

IMPACTS OF BOULDERING

Bouldering as a sport places a considerable strain on our OSMP lands (all lands for that matter). While in search of new areas, climbers tend to travel the path of least resistance. This results in the formation of undesignated footpaths, where vegetation has been worn away by the passage of many feet.

Undesignated paths kill plants, some of which are rare or endangered. They increase runoff, cause erosion and deprive nearby plants of crucial water. They also aid the spread of noxious invasive weeds.

To prepare boulders for climbing, some people "garden," or scrub lichen, moss and plants off the rock. They may clear the area surrounding boulder problems, trampling and crushing the delicate vegetation with crash pads. It could take *hundreds of years* for slow-growing lichens to grow back!

Besides being a violation of OSMP regulations, this activity further degrades the resource. Many plants found in moist rock crevices are extremely rare; some have yet to be identified. By destroying them, we all lose a precious resource.

V-GRADES

Grades are a measure of the chore ahead. In this guide, rest assured that the lowest grade ever mentioned for a given problem has been used. This is in no way meant to detract from your opinion of yourself as a boulderer; it is merely a reflection of the somewhat stiff standards already in place in Colorado. Obviously this doesn't hold true for every problem, so you will find some variance in the grades.

Grades reflect the subjective nature of bouldering, an excellent quality in and of itself. If you have a hard time with a certain grade, consider ascending the problem before you start bickering. Remember that the grade is the least significant part of the bouldering experience. You need only stand back from the rock, take in the beauty of your surroundings and chill out a moment to realize the absurdity of a single insignificant grade.

STAR RATINGS

One criticism of the first book was that it contained too many 3-star problems, detracting from the mega-classic status of certain problems by lumping them in with the merely excellent. We've added a star in the hopes of creating just such a distinction, but again, quality ratings are completely subjective.

No stars = Dirty or not especially interesting.
* = Better than average, a pretty good boulder problem.
** = Puts a smile on your face if you send it but upsets you if you don't.
*** = An exceptional boulder problem, well worth the effort. Two scoops please!
**** = One of Colorado's best, an "irrefutable" "classic."

PRECAUTIONS

Bouldering is an inherently dangerous activity rife with the opportunity to get a boo-boo. You can break your femur or radius or coccyx while bouldering! If you boulder alone on suspect rock, realize that you might be rolling the dice. If you're fortunate enough to have competent spotters, then use them to your full advantage. The same goes for crash pads, which you can force your sub-men to carry if necessary.

APPROXIMATIONS/DISTANCES:

Take all approximate distances in this book with a huge handful of salt! While listing the hundreds of boulders in the guide, we often resorted to eyeballing the distances between boulders. These distances are measured in feet or yards or minutes, and may differ from your estimations. If you cannot find a boulder, consider the fact that 10, 25, 50 or 100 yards differs substantially from one climber to the next. Take your time and retrace your steps, check the guide for additional information (i.e. what direction the boulder lies in) and keep the photo or topo handy to aid you in discerning the location of the next rock upon which to dash both your ego and your flesh.

SYMBOLS AND ABBREVIATIONS:

Bad Landing, Highball, Sit Down Start: Bad landings are indicated by a broken ankle emblem. We have used this icon for problems on uneven talus, logs or a sloping hillside. Also if the fall can be unbalanced due to the body's movement during a dyno, heel hook or possible hold breakage. For a highball problem an ambulance symbol is used. This designation is used for problems 15 feet or higher—although a few problems may only be a mere 14 ft 2 in. Sit Down Start is sds in problem descriptions.

 Highball: You might need alternative transportation from the crag if you crater.

 Bad Landing: Roots, rocks, uneven terrain, or other factors create a dangerous landing.

  Both: Fogettaboutit. Don't bother falling.

COMPASS DIRECTIONS:

Problems are described using every compass direction. If a problem indicates the southwest arete, that means the arete somewhere within the area of the south and west faces. If unsure, read the problem description and check the photo or topo to narrow down the correct problem. Carrying a compass is highly recommended in remote or newly developed areas.

ORIENTATION:

For problems using left and right descriptions, the orientation is always as one faces the boulder or cliff. The orientation can be difficult to ascertain in gaps and chasms, so look carefully at the photo, topo and other problem descriptions for the same boulder.

PHOTO / TOPO NUMBERS:

Problem numbers on photos and topos are not always directly in front of a problem due to trees, bushes or other boulders blocking a clear view. In this instance use the photo or topo to find the boulder, then use the problem's description to locate the correct problem. When a photo or topo is not used for a boulder, use the closest photographed or topoed boulder—orient yourself then read the boulder's description to locate it and the problems.

ACKNOWLEDGEMENTS

The guidebook authors would like to thank the following companies/individuals for their invaluable help in making this book a reality:

Metolius Mountain Products for all the great gear and bomber crashpads, Cordless for their killer pads, La Sportiva and Five Ten for their superlative footwear, Adam Avery for his unyielding hospitality and delicious beers, Vic's Espresso, The Hungry Toad, Jim Belcer, Mike Brooks (www.frontrangebouldering.com), Josh Deuto, Jay Droeger, John Dunn, Herm Feissner, Mike Freischlag, Charles Fryberger, Chris Gopelrud, Naomi Guy, Tom Hanson, Bob Horan, Jonathan Houck, Haven Iverson, Eric Johnson, Greg Johnson, Ken Kenney, Colin Lantz, Charles Lintott, Eric Pals, Pete Peacock, Alison Rockwell, Chip Ruckgaber, Burton Stoner of OSMP, Bart Streghe, Trixie Tartasky, Matt Tiwonowski, Brad Tomlin, Tim Toula, Dave Whaley, Pat Wilde, Pete Zoller and anyone we might have forgotten.

STATE MAP OF COLORADO

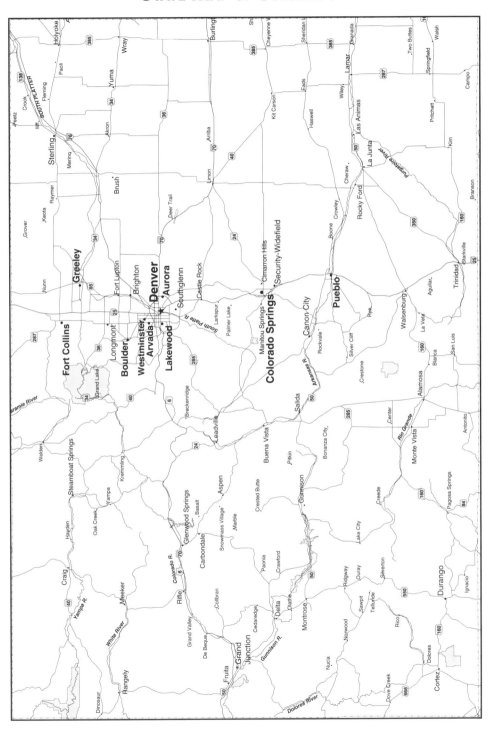

TABLE OF CONTENTS

METOLIUS BOULDERING

metoliusclimbing.com

Front Range

GETTING AROUND THE FRONT RANGE

Colorado's Front Range is the most densely populated and fastest growing region in the state. If you are unfamiliar with the region, a detailed map is recommended for travel to the various climbing areas. As mentioned elsewhere, this guidebook assumes a basic knowledge of the state and/or the resources to find small cities. The following map is provided for those who have forgotten their state map at home or are suffering from momentary geographic amnesia. It is assumed that the authors' written descriptions in conjunction with the included maps will be adequate to locate the specific climbing areas.

Jay Droeger on The Seam   photo: Phillip Benningfield

LUMPY RIDGE

The newfound boulders on Lumpy are a godsend. They are numerous and secluded. Two fine gems, The Cube and The French Fry were added to the tally only in the past two years. The blocks are extremely large with high finishes and superb, albeit thin, problems. Any session on Lumpy would be incomplete without a visit to these boulders as well as the new Pear Boulders.

PEAR BOULDERS

The boulders listed here have previously been ignored because the other Pear Boulders (see the original Colorado Bouldering) are far more appealing and aesthetic. The advantage of these new blocks is a wider variety of problems and more bouldering concentrated in a smaller area.

Directions: Walk on the main trail headed west from the information kiosk. Stay on the lower trail that hugs the wooden fence. Continue on this trail for 15-20 minutes, and pass The World's Greatest Boulder (on left of trail with cracks on the northwest face), and go through a wooden gate. The Pear climber's trail is a short distance on the right (from the Pear sign look north and the boulders are visible). Walk up the Pear trail 150 yards (the main Pear Boulders are to the left) then head due east 100 yards.

SCOOP BOULDER

A smooth boulder with a black scooped-out east face. A seam splits the right side of the east face.

1. The Seam V6 ** 🖐️

Climb the right-leaning seam on the east face.

2. V1

The northeast arete, up jugs to a mantle finish.

3. V0-V2 *

A selection of slabs can be done on the west face. Expect thin edging for tips and boots.

HORIZONTALS

Just northeast 25 feet from Scoop Boulder is a boulder with a horizontal crack across the northwest and south faces.

1. V1 * 🖐️

The left problem from a low start under the roof on the northwest face.

2. V1 ** 🖐️

The right problem under the roof that climbs to the southwest arete then up the short slab.

HIGHLY HORIZONTAL BLOCK

Uphill to the north 20 yards is a block with horizontal cracks along its south face.

1. V0 *

The right side of the south face off the good undercling flake. Exit around the corner to avoid a terrifying top-out.

SCRUNCH BLOCK

Just to the right of Highly Horizontal is a small block with a steep southeast side.

2. V0 *

The easy slab directly right of Highly Horizontal.

ADDITIONAL PROBLEM
V2

The right-trending seam by the big pine just to the northwest of Scoop Boulder. Pictured right.

THE CUBE

A beautiful block with problems on every side. The Cube can be used as a warm-up boulder but you need to feel comfortable on high problems that begin at V2. Perfect landings and memorable problems define this extraordinary block.

Directions: Walk west on the main trail, skirting the kiosk on its left. Continue along the trail (a wooden fence is left of the trail) past the sign and gate for entering Rocky Mountain National Park. After passing through the gate continue past the Pear Trail (heads up to the right) and past three blocks on the right (the Pear Boulders—see Colorado Bouldering). The trail stays headed west and goes up a slight incline with erosion steps. Pass a faint drainage coming in from the cliffs then follow the left side of the drainage towards Thunder Buttress. The Cube is found approximately 250 yards up in the woods and on the hillside directly below the low large roof on Thunder Buttress.

SOUTH FACE

A tall slabby face with a small tree blocking access to the tallest section of the face.

1. V2 *

On the left side on the south face is an arete dividing the south and west faces. Long reaches and friable feet are the rule.

2. V3 **
Start just right of the tree and move right to a good set of edges. Move straight up to the high seam and micro edges. Escape right to the small huecos.

East Face
The most uneventful section of the block.

3. V0
On the left side of the east face is a small bulge to start then ledges to the top.

4. V1 *
Start low on a big left-facing sidepull then up to an obvious sloper below the roof. Exit left of the roof.

North Face
The cold side of the block, facing Thunder Buttress.

5. V2 **
Start on the corner between the north and east faces, then follow the arete to a long reach over the lip.

6. V3 **
Just right of #5 is a high set of edges. Start on these edges and throw to the right-leaning arete. Hidden edges appear to soothe the worried mind. A V8 link can be done starting on #7 and traversing in from the right.

7. V1 ***
A superb line climbing up the middle of the north face from the jugs at arm's reach. Utilize holds in the left-facing dihedral and exit either right or left at the top.

8. V?
Climb the extremely small sloping edges right of #7.

9. V3 **
Starts with a jump to the sloping shelf on the right of the north face then up good edges.

West Face
A golden face littered with edges.

10. V0
Climb the left side of the face up good edges to the sloping top-out.

11. V4 ***

The direct line, up the middle of the west face, on positive edges. A fantastic vertical affair that requires far more technique and thought than power.

SPRING BOULDERS

These two blocks are located 200 yards west of The Cube. Walk on a faint game trail due west but head uphill ever so slightly. The first block with problems will be directly east of a spring and the other is easily seen 40 yards to the west.

SPRING BOULDER

The boulder right by the spring; it has not been well traveled but offers a couple of intriguing problems on the west face.

V0

Several V0s climb the lichen-covered slabs on the south face.

WESTERN SPRING BOULDER

This block, with a tall white slab on the west face, is 40 yards west of the spring.

1. V1 **

Follow the right-facing dihedral up the tall slab on the west face.

2. V3 ***

The traverse across the south face from right to left. Ends with a throw to the lip before the west face. An extension traverse continues along the thin seam on the west face.

3. V2

A low start on the left end of the seam on the east face to a sloping right-trending ramp. A traverse along the seam to #4 is hard.

4. V1 *

The right problem on the east face that climbs through the questionable white and black holds to jugs over the top.

THE FRENCH FRY

When it comes to getting psyched for a new boulder this beauty fits the bill. The boulder is shaped like a french-fry but offers so much more than grease; you get tip-shredding crisp edges and fright as well. The south face is a mere 12 feet wide but the east and west faces are nearly 60 feet long and covered in edges made to bring smiley faces to the tips and pure joy to the day.

Directions: Be very, very patient when trying to locate this block! It is obscure and easy to miss on the massive hillside. The block is located below the left side of The Pear and can be reached from The Cube by walking due east along the hillside approximately 250 yards (look for the golden south face). The block can also be reached by walking up the Pear Trail 200 yards then west into the woods for another 150 yards.

SOUTH FACE

The golden 12-foot wide face with a gorgeous right arete.

1. V1

Climb the ledges on the left of the south face. Be ever mindful of loose, dirty rock.

EAST FACE

A 60-foot long gray and tan face with blank granite on the left and tons of problems from the middle to the far right section of the wall.

2. V5 *

The leftmost line, before the trees, with a flat landing. Starts with the right hand using the left starting hold on #3 then up and left. Expect extremely thin edges to a hard move to reach the top.

3. V4 **

An awesome line starting off two positive edges then up to a right-facing sidepull then the high ledge and higher exit.

4. V2 *

Start on the ramp and climb the good left-hand edges and atrocious right-hand sidepulls.

5. Cryin' Out Loud V5 ***

Start low on two perfect crimpers then move right on progressively sharper and more painful edges and a difficult top-out.

West Face

A long slabby wall with far more problems than listed here. All problems are 20-plus feet tall and lichen covered.

6. V1*

The rightmost line starting right of the corner system and following the slabby ledges to the top.

Ned Harris on Cryin' Out Loud   photo: Jay Droeger

ROCKY MOUNTAIN NATIONAL PARK

You've heard the spray—just where are all those good, high-country boulders? Interest in Rocky Mountain National Park's alpine bouldering potential has grown recently, perhaps as a result of increasingly hot Front Range summers and global warming. Crash pads have made jagged, talus landings viable and team spotting has opened up previously unthinkable highballs on the large, varied erratics that dot the landscape of this vast preserve.

Most areas require a bit of an approach and are subject to alpine weather conditions. The bouldering areas are spread out, making it difficult to visit more than one cluster per session and temperatures can vary greatly depending on weather conditions. Bring a rain jacket, do your best not to walk on tundra, and keep a low profile. Some areas have not been included in this book due to impact/access issues; remember, you're in a National Park—stay on existing trails, respect re-vegetation closures, obey ALL the rules and be courteous to Rangers and non-climbers alike.

HOLLOWELL PARK UPDATE (KB BOULDER)

This low-lying, south-facing picnic area on the road to Bear Lake is one of the warmer, drier venues in the park. As such, it's possible to climb here year around, though midday summer temperatures can be hot. With a little bit of vision, the large blocks and walls on the hill above the picnic area should provide some challenging highballs. In the meantime, sample the handful of choice problems on the aesthetic KB Boulder.

Directions: Take Highway 36 west from Estes Park to the Beaver Meadows Entrance Station to Rocky Mountain National Park. Pay your $10 (or better yet, arrive before 8am, when the Entrance Station opens, and pay nothing!) and drive 0.2 miles to a junction. Take a left (south) onto the Bear Lake Road, which you follow 3.6 miles from the junction to a right turn into Hollowell Park. Drive to the west end of the parking lot and park. Follow the foot/horse path west out of the parking lot, passing a corral and a large, fluted boulder (the Carcass Boulder) on your right about five minutes up the trail. Five more minutes of walking takes you over a small, forested shoulder and down onto the east edge of a large flat meadow. From here cut right up the hill 50 yards to reach the boulder, a large, gray egg in the trees. Approach time: ten minutes.

KB BOULDER

Combining this boulder with all the problems on the Hollowell Park Boulder (five minutes east of the parking area) makes for a good granite circuit. Though not super-extensive, this secluded block has wonderful stone and good landings. Bring your crimpin' fingers, G!

1. Snizzle Sticks V7 **
The leftmost line, from a sds, past small crimps in the faint corners. V2 from the stand-up.

2. Thai Sticks V5 ** 😎
This is the center line on the wall. Sds on a good rail and move up and right onto the clean, gray face, where hidden crimpers await. A mere V3 if you opt for the left exit.

3. KB V8 **** 😎
Gymnastic, continuous and thuggy. Start at the good lock in the finger crack (you may need a cheater stone), move left into the faint scoop on edges then work the "V."

4. Crack V4 *
The awkward finger crack behind the tree, starting on #3 but continuing up the crack.

CAMP DICK

Naomi Guy on the Alpen Glow Boulder   photo: Jay Droeger

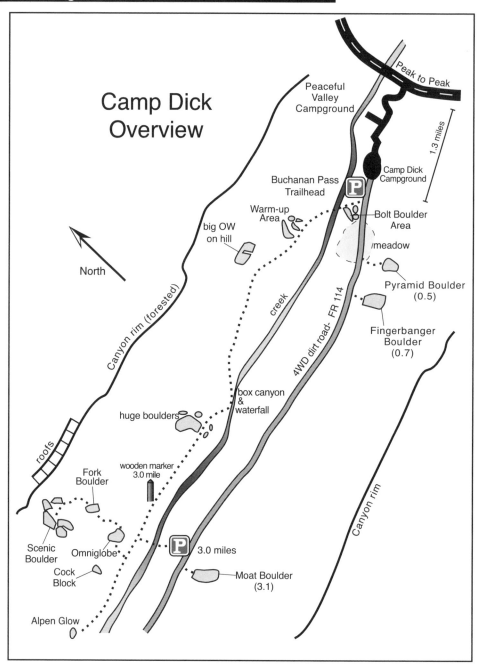

Camp Dick Overview

Peak to Peak

Peaceful Valley Campground

1.3 miles

Camp Dick Campground

Buchanan Pass Trailhead

P

Bolt Boulder Area

Warm-up Area

big OW on hill

meadow

North

Pyramid Boulder (0.5)

Canyon rim (forested)

creek

4WD dirt road- FR 114

Fingerbanger Boulder (0.7)

box canyon & waterfall

huge boulders

roofs

wooden marker 3.0 mile

Fork Boulder

Canyon rim

Scenic Boulder

Omniglobe

P

3.0 miles

Cock Block

Moat Boulder (3.1)

Alpen Glow

CAMP DICK

Although people have known about the granite boulders littering this valley for years, it wasn't until the summer of 2000 that anything decent was discovered. The untrammeled alpine setting and the high quality of the compact granite combine to make "The Dick" a superb bouldering experience, marred only by the scattered nature of the boulders. For those who don't mind a little hiking, the Omniglobe Area, in its idyllic aspen grove setting, has the highest concentration of problems. With countless boulders littering the dense, primordial forest that blankets the canyon, Camp Dick offers the promise of new bouldering for years to come.

"The Dick" is best during summer and into fall, as it can be quite snowy even into June, and the shadier rocks on the southeast side of the canyon take a long time to dry. Though the drive from Boulder is only 20 miles, it's 20 of the steepest, windiest miles you'll ever drive, so allow yourself an hour to get there and another hour to hike/drive to the more remote areas.

Directions: Heading north on Broadway out of Boulder, take a left (west) onto Old Stage Road, the last light in town (all mileage is given from this point). Drive 4.5 miles to the junction with the Lefthand Canyon Road, then take a left. At 7.2 miles stay right on the road to Jamestown (don't go left to Ward), passing through Jamestown at 10.2 miles. At 16.9 miles the road ends at the Peak-to-Peak Highway. Turn right, follow the road down a large hill and take a left at the bottom of the dip (18.5 miles). If you pass the sign for Peaceful Valley on the left you've gone 50 yards too far (Peaceful Valley is located on the Peak-to-Peak Highway between Ward and Hwy 7).

Follow the narrow paved road west into the valley, passing the Peaceful Valley Campground and the Camp Dick Campground before the paved road ends at the Buchanan Pass Trailhead (19.8 miles). For the Trail Boulders (The Traverse, Warm-up Area, Omniglobe, Cock Block and Jumbotron), park here and follow the signs for the Buchanan Pass Trail. For the Roadside Boulders (Bolt Boulder, Pyramid Boulder, Fingerbanger Boulder and Moat Boulder), walk or drive west up the very rough four-wheel drive road, FR 114. This road can also be used to access the Trail Boulders.

BOLT BOULDER AREA

Head up the 4WD road from the parking just past the Buchanan Pass Trail. The boulders are on the right. This set of three blocks provides the easiest access with problems ranging from V0 to V7.

Bolt Boulder Problem V5

This fragile, loose, low-quality problem ascends the bolted line facing down valley (east).

BEHIND THE BOLT BOULDER

This is the tallest block with problems facing the creek.

1. UK Hockey Night V6 **

Climb the left arete on the north face to the high ramp's right side then up.

2. Legend of the Drunken Master V7 **

Climb the faint corner right of the black streak with a huge move to reach the summit plateau.

3. V3 ***

Ascend the superb solid sidepulls to a straight up finish from a pinch.

4. V2 *

Climb the shorter right side of the north face to a slopey finish.

5. Roadie V0

This easy slab problem sits directly adjacent to the road and climbs to a jug at mid-height then the top.

6. V3

The thin slab immediatley left of #5.

THE TRAVERSE BOULDER

A lone block that rests on the right side of the Buchanan Pass Trail after a brief 300 yard stroll west from the bridge over the creek.

1. The Traverse V4 ***

An excellent sloper problem beginning from the slopers just left of the rounded sidepulls that lead up the block's middle. A V8 traverse begins on the boulder's far left side and continues through the V4.

2. V3

On the southwest side begin from a flat ledge or undercling or nasty kneebar and climb up the open "V," staying to the right to a jug at mid-height.

3. Variations V2-V5

Same start as #2 and contrive a multitude of entertaining problems.

WARM-UP AREA

This conglomeration of tall blocks is located 100 yards past The Traverse on the trail's right side. It is impossible to miss these boulders. Problems range from numerous V0 slabs to a couple of obscure traverses and sit-downs that reach V5 in difficulty. These blocks are certainly the best choice for novice boulderers; as well as those who are afraid of highballs, desperate affairs, and long drawn-out approaches.

Mike Freischlag on a V0

Roadside Boulders

Directions: If you have a burly 4WD vehicle and don't mind driving three miles an hour, then zero your odometer out at the start of the road (FDR 114) and redneck on up to the boulders—be aware that driving to the Omniglobe takes only marginally less time than hiking, and is easily twice as annoying.

The Pyramid Boulder

Well-hidden in a thick pine forest, this aptly named boulder is a good tick in the summer, as it stays well-shaded all day. Though not extensive, the bouldering here is excellent. Drive 0.5 miles up the road from the trailhead and park in a large meadow, directly across from a large block with an obvious offwidth crack, high on the canyon wall to the right (north). Walk 40 yards off the road due south along a faint track to reach the boulder.

1. V0
Start matched on a ledge on the far left, gaston a crystal, and top out left. V2 if you start in the crack and grab the crystal with your left hand.

2. Treetop Flyer V5 ***
Follow the right-leaning crack up the immaculate white face. Airy and involved.

3. Mr. Clean V7 ** Photo on right
Harder from a sds start on the left (north) side, this prow can also be climbed on the right at V3. Cool moves on good, black stone.

4. Le Banging du Fingers V3 *
A pumpy, left to right traverse across the west face of the boulder, beginning on #3 and finishing far right on crimps. Somewhat mossy.

5. Dicey and Dirty V2
The high, licheny slab on the tall face right of #4. Use caution, especially up high.

6. V0
The detached flake veering right, then straight up.

Fingerbanger Boulder

This 20-foot high, square-shaped block is roughly 0.7 miles from the trailhead. Park on the right in a small campsite. The boulder sits 30 feet south of the road, offering decent, though crimpy, warm-ups on its south side and higher, harder lines on the impressive east face. A good, sunny hang with perfect landings.

South Face
1. Pete's Party Pudding V1
Take a small crimp with your right hand and fire over the lip.

2. Matt's Dirty Fingers V3
The faint seam in a black streak near the middle of the wall.

3. Slopus, Slopus V0+
The slopey, rounded arete on the right side of the wall.

EAST FACE
4. V2
The funkus left side. Climb past the diagonaling horizontal and onto the mossy slab.

5. Drop Kick Murphy V4 *
Up the obvious thin finger crack, moving right onto the bulge to top out. V5 from the lowest holds in the crack. Beware the loose chockstone!

6. V10 ****
Shares a start with #7, then move left up crimps and pinches to the apex of the boulder.

7. Le Fingerbanger V7 ***
Start on a crimp rail at head height where the boulder bends north, then slap your way past crimps on the rounded prow, moving left to finish. The exit has claimed at least one ankle!

8. Pattycake V6 ***
From the Fingerbanger start move right into the overhanging black scoop. V3 from a stand-up start on the block. Slopey, technical, excellent.

Drop Kick Murphy

9. Mantle Panties V1
On the uninspiring west face of the boulder. Mantle two crimps at head height then punch it up the 20-foot mossy slab.

MR. SMOOTHY BOULDER (NOT PICTURED)
This is a funky, highly polished (read: blank) slab of rock about 300 yards up the road from the Fingerbanger Boulder. It sits just off the road on the left and offers a trio of slabby but unique problems.

1. Mr. Smoothy V3 *
Follow the left-trending sloper rail.

2. Mr. Touchy V3
The arete on the right side of the wall.

3. Mr. Feely V3 *
The obvious crimpy face.

THE MOAT BOULDER

There is a distinctive swampy moat at the base of the north-west face of this gigantic block. The rock is every bit as good as on Fingerbanger Boulder. The highball V4 on its east face makes for a great excursion.

Directions: From the Omniglobe parking at 3.0 miles, walk up the road another 100 yards until you hit a series of log steps. Head left into the forest 20 feet from the steps to the obvious, square-cut boulder.

1. Mikey's Traverse V0 *
There is a boulder leaning against the back of the Moat Boulder. This is a right to left lip traverse of this boulder.

2. V4 ***
One of the best problems at "The Dick." Begin in the middle of the east face and cruise left past plates and flakes to a stimulating finish.

3. V6 **
The crimpy, gymnastic prow formed by the meeting of the east and north faces. Hard on the fingers.

4. V5 **
The first problem above the moat on the front (north) face. Start on a slopey rail and jump to higher holds in the black scoop above.

5. V6 **
Begin above the right edge of the moat and step onto a glassy slab, then move up and right to a ramp behind a log leaning against the boulder. Slippery and technical, this problem is V3 if you start on the ramp.

6. V1
The small, unremarkable slab right of the dead log.

The Hardman on Put Some Hair Around It   photo: Phillip Benningfield

TRAIL BOULDERS

Directions: Drive up the hideously rocky four-wheel drive road to 3.0 miles and park where you can. Follow a small cairned trail northwest across the river to the Buchanan Pass Trail, where you intersect the faint track to the Omniglobe.

Otherwise, walk roughly an hour up the Buchanan Pass Trail, passing a 3-mile marker on a brown, three-foot-high wooden post on your right. From here, continue up the trail another 5-10 minutes, passing eight (count em', 8) diamond-shaped, blue trail markers nailed to the trees. Twenty feet before the ninth diamond head back and right on a climber's trail (look for small cairns) to the Omniglobe, which is one minute to the north. If you come across an obvious and very filthy 20-foot-high rock just left of the trail, you need to backtrack about 100 yards. The Cock Block is roughly 100 yards up-canyon from here (northwest) through the trees.

From the north face of the Omniglobe follow a faint track northish, then west up the hill to reach the Fork Boulder (2 min) and the Scenic Boulders (3 min).

The Jumbotron requires a bit more of an approach. Drive another quarter mile past the Omniglobe parking and park in the lot at the end of the 4WD road. Cross the creek via the bridge and head down-canyon (right) three or four minutes on the Buchanan Pass Trail until you reach a large clearing. Head 150 yards uphill (towards a talus field) along a faint trail (possible cairns) then head right (down-canyon) towards the grouping of big boulders just below the cliff line. Approach time from the parking lot: 20-25 minutes.

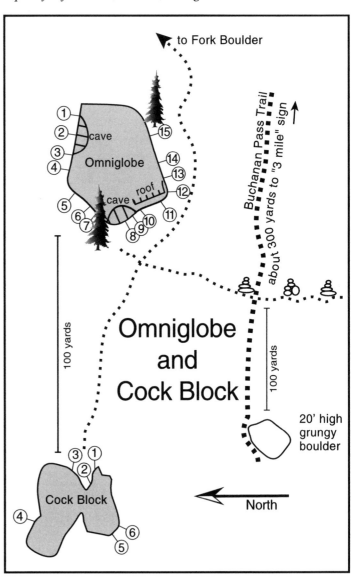

36

THE OMNIGLOBE BOULDER

This perfect cube of white and grey granite is surely one of the "Best in Colorado." From 20-foot-long cavey desperates to 20-foot-plus technical highballs on vertical, white stone, this boulder has it all—unparalleled bouldering in a secluded, forested setting.

NORTH CAVE

1. The Dogfight V6 *

From a low undercling in the bottom left of the cave reel left out the chossy crack to the lip. A slightly contrived V8 moves straight up from the start of this problem.

2. Put Some Hair Around It V8 ***

An exemplary boulder problem: powerful moves on perfect rock. Either begin low as for #1 (V8+) or start standing up on good laybacks at chest height, punching past slopey ramps to the triangular apex of the cave. Can be started from #3 at V9.

3. Schwagg V6 **

Almost as good as its neighbor. Sds low on the cave's right margin at a big pinch, then punch past crimps and a glued flake to a difficult lip encounter.

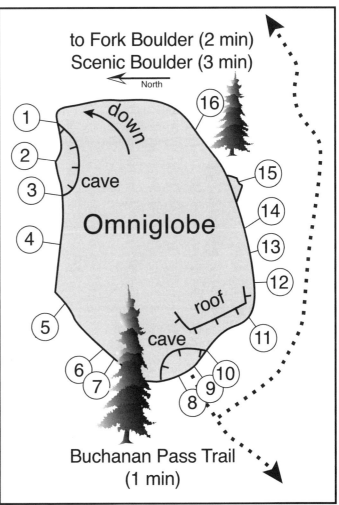

to Fork Boulder (2 min)
Scenic Boulder (3 min)

← North

Omniglobe

down

cave

cave

roof

Buchanan Pass Trail
(1 min)

West Face

4. V3 *

Begin just right of #3 and move past the double overlaps in the black streak, topping out just left of a patch of heather. Can also be started on #5.

5. V1 * **

Begin at the downward-pointing "V" and work up the 20-foot tall white face on perfect incuts. Face climbing at its best!

6. V2 **

Start on a jug at waist height then grunt your way past a series of faint, left-facing liebacks. Tricky.

7. Theo's Problem V6 **

Start on #6 then climb the high, thin face next to the tree.

South Cave

Problems 8-10 can be finished out the hanging, black prow of The Maxi Pad for full value. Alternately, rock over right onto the ledge and either jump down or head up a V0 dihedral above (subtract one V-grade, you lightweight!).

8. The Maxi Pad V4 **

Sds at a good rail running across the south cave, then work left and up into crimps, traversing out the hanging prow.

9. Cleaner's Call V7 **

Start as for #8 and head directly up on tiny, painful crimpers to the sloping lip. Powerful.

10. Sweet Emily V8 **

Sds matching on a three-foot high jug, three feet right of #9, then up past a pocket into slopers.

Southeast Face

11. V2 **

Either start on a slopey rail directly under the right side of the large upper roof or begin four feet further right on an undercling. Thrutch your way past the bottom, then cruise straight out the right side of the large roof on perfect jugs.

12. V4 ** 🚗

Begin as for #11 but head right onto a rounded prow after the opening moves, climbing carefully around a large, loose block to top out. Great moves in a great position.

EAST FACE

13. V5 *** 🚗

The obvious thin crack that begins in a corner and runs up the right side of the prow. Technical, ferocious and scary.

14. Project *** 🚗

Directly up the east face on the tiny crimps that litter the seam-ridden, impeccable black stone.

15. Raggedy Man V4 ** 🚗

Start on a small rock below the right-leaning ramp. Toss for the ramp then head up behind the tree. V6 from the lowest possible crimps.

16. Raggedy Ann V0+ *

A decent little warm-up problem out blocky holds in a small corner behind the tree.

THE COCK BLOCK

With a handful of completed problems and potential for a few new classics, the Cock Block offers a good companion area to the nearby Omniglobe. Approach by hiking 100 yards up-canyon from the Omniglobe through the trees in a direction more or less parallel with the Buchanan Pass Trail. Patience may be required to locate this hidden block.

1. V1

Climb jugs up and right to a scary top-out.

2. Dick V3 *

Start on the right side of the cave and move up and left.

3. Don't Call Me Dick V5 *

Sds. Inspired by the VRG's "Don't Call Me Dude," and nearly as classic to boot.

4. Dick's Slab V4 ** 🚗

A great, highball slab problem.

5. Dick's Other Slab V2 **

Another engaging slab for those of you with twinkle-toes!

6. Dick's Arete V4 *

A fun arete climb.

Jim Belcer on I Love Dick photo: Jay Droeger

Fork Boulder

1. Ball That Jack V5 **** 😊
This problem climbs the obvious, overhanging block that faces north on your way to the Scenic Boulders. Work past jugs and slopers into the faint scoop in the middle of the rock, then huck for the lip. Photo on right.

The Scenic Boulders

Just uphill from Fork Boulder and the Omniglobe, this complicated cluster of boulders offers a great range of moderates and desperates as well as an awesome view up-valley to the mighty Indian Peaks Wilderness. The rock here is more metamorphic than granitic, lending itself to dynamic moves up solid squarecuts, on interesting gray stone.

The Parallelogram

This is the small, slick-walled boulder forming the left wall of a corridor on the southeast side of the grotto. It offers fun moderates.

1. Lip Traverse V1 *
Traverse the lip of the boulder from left to right, then back. A good warm-up.

2. Face V3 *
Straight up crimps in the middle of the wall.

3. Tree Jam V2 *
Begin on holds near the aspen tree, then head up the right side of the wall. A hand jam against the tree trunk is considered "on."

The Uber-Pyramid

This gigantic boulder/spire sits just uphill (west) of the Parallelogram, forming the right wall of the corridor.

4. Big Richard V1 ** 😊
On the southeast face of this 30-foot-high pyramidal block is this highball. Begin low on a rail then work right and up to a high, licheny top-out.

5. Little Richard V1
Climb out the roof/prow in the corridor formed by the neighboring Parallelogram.

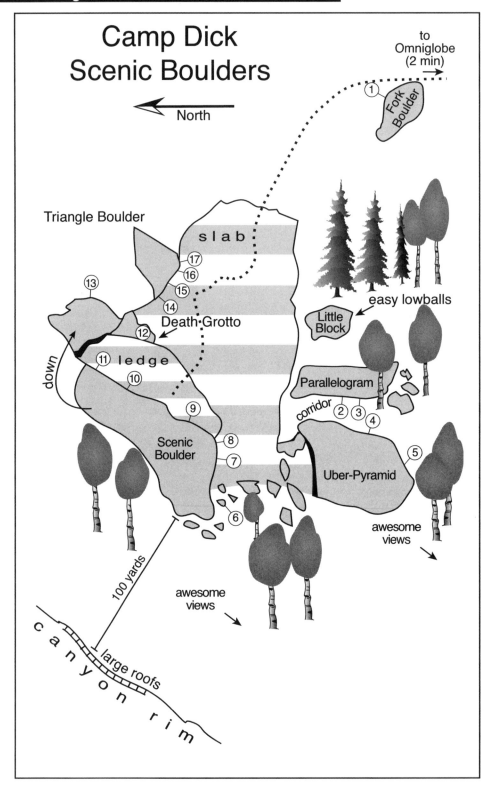

Camp Dick
Scenic Boulders

← North

to
Omniglobe
(2 min)

① Fork Boulder

Triangle Boulder

s l a b

⑰
⑯
⑮
⑬
⑭

Death Grotto

⑫

down

⑪ l e d g e

⑩

⑨

Scenic
Boulder

⑧

⑦

⑥

easy lowballs

Little Block

Parallelogram

corridor ② ③ ④

⑤

Uber-Pyramid

awesome views

awesome views

100 yards

large roofs

c a n y o n   r i m

SCENIC BOULDER

This excellent boulder is the centerpiece of the area, both spiritually and geographically. It is the long, vertical to overhanging wall located at the back (west) end of the grotto, and offers a fine array of stiff problems.

6. The Sub-Par Bouldering 🌀

Three not-so-noteworthy problems climb out the short left side of the south-facing, overhanging wave in the aspen grove.

7. I Love Dick V7 *** 🖐

Yes, you do. Either start on opposing sidepulls at head height and reef up the middle of the wave, or begin low in a hand crack for the full V8 excursion. Bring lots of pads for the uneven, rocky landing. See intro photo to Scenic Boulders.

8. Project V? **** 🚗

Out the prow right of #7. Will be exceptional when completed.

9. Swallow This V5 *** 😎   Photo top right

Follow a thin finger seam in a left-facing corner, then realm up the beautiful face above. Technical and insidious.

10. Easy Highball V2 * 😎   Photo just right

This would get an extra star if the rock were better. Begin right above the best landing on the platform and work past pinches and jugs—treat the holds gently!

11. We Gotta Save Them Critters V5 ** 😎 🌀

Above the right margin of the platform, punch up the crack, bust right to slopey holds, then head straight up on edges. Scary.

DEATH GROTTO

This is the tight (read: dangerous) corridor/chimney just to the right of Scenic Boulder.

12. Death by Dick V2 **

Climb the obtuse corner, with its perfect pink and white stone, on the corridor's right wall. Begin near the outside of the corridor and work left into the corner. Don't fall!

13. Finessa V3 **

On the back side of Death Grotto. Start on jagged blocks and crimp your way up the orange veneer on the 13-foot face.

TRIANGLE BOULDER

This is the small, triangle-shaped block just below Death Grotto. It is the lowest, rightmost boulder in the cluster as you approach.

14. Warm-up Arete V0 *

Realming up the crisp arete. Harder if done from the left side.

15. V1 *

Begin in the middle of the face right of the arete, then work back to the arete at 10 feet. A fun warm-up on positive holds.

16. Little Jack Horner V0 *

The obvious corner to the right. Harder if you start low, in the monkey pit.

17. Uncle Bumbly V1

Begin right of the corner, grab an incut on the left, heel hook, and wind your way up the fractured blocks.

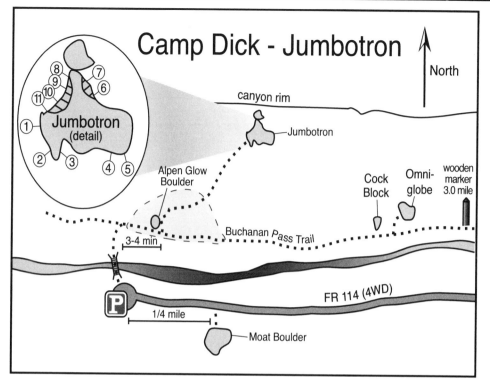

THE JUMBOTRON

If your legs aren't tired by the time you reach The Omniglobe then pack up your pads and head on up to The Jumbotron, an isolated, house-sized block further up the canyon. This boulder sits in a sunny, warm spot, making it a good choice on colder days or when the wind is screaming down out of the high country. Potential for new problems seemingly abounds.

1. Get to the Point V3 ***
Start low and left and climb along the right-leaning roof to the point of the arete. This is the first problem you encounter upon reaching the boulder. Problems are described in a counter-clockwise direction from here.

2. V2 *
Climb the arete up and left.

3. V4 **
Start in the back of the cave then move up and left.

4. Creaky Slab V3 *
Realm up the highball slab on creaky, disconcerting edges.

5. V0 *
Climb out the small roof via good jugs. This problem is a nice warm-up.

Note: #6 and #7 are in a hole on the northwest side of the boulder.

6. Dead Teletubbies V5 ***

This is the obvious line of slopers out the left side of the hole, off-routing the left arete for your hands. Tricky.

7. Uncle Mike's Late Show V4

Aka "The Nasty Crimpy Thing." Climb straight out of the hole on painful sharpies. Ouch!

Note: #8 through #11 climb out of a similar hole on the other side of the boulder abutting The Jumbotron to the right.

8. Corner V2 *

Tackle the easy corner on the left side of the hole.

9. Ken's Party Pudding V7 **

A hard, crimpy line that starts down in the hole just right of #8.

10. The Orifice V2 ***

A classic thuggy problem that climbs out of the hole on positive grips.

11. Dick's Party Pudding V4 *

The rightmost line in the hole, moving straight up past sidepulls and crimps.

ALPEN GLOW BOULDER

A relatively easy block sitting alone in an alpine meadow with the most inspiring backdrop of the Dick repertoire. Problems range from V0 to V5 on cool swirly rock (individual problems not listed). A good block for those afraid of the "Dick's" usual highballs.

Directions: From the Omniglobe, continue up the Buchanan Pass Trail for a few minutes, into a meadow (1/2 mile). It is impossible to miss the boulder as it sits trailside.

LION'S DEN

Naomi Guy on the Cougar Cache Wall   photo: Matt Samet

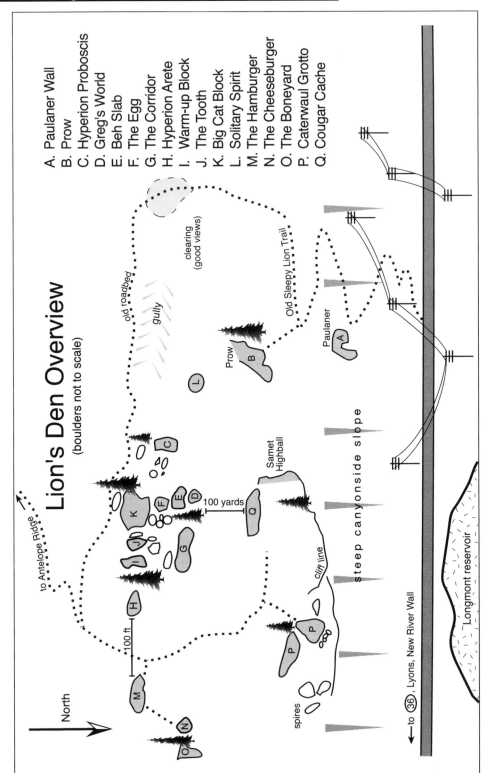

Lion's Den Overview
(boulders not to scale)

A. Paulaner Wall
B. Prow
C. Hyperion Proboscis
D. Greg's World
E. Beh Slab
F. The Egg
G. The Corridor
H. Hyperion Arete
I. Warm-up Block
J. The Tooth
K. Big Cat Block
L. Solitary Spirit
M. The Hamburger
N. The Cheeseburger
O. The Boneyard
P. Caterwaul Grotto
Q. Cougar Cache

old roadbed

clearing
(good views)

gully

Old Sleepy Lion Trail

Paulaner

Prow

L

to Antelope Ridge

North

C

F
E
D

K

J
J

G

I

100 yards

Q

Samet
Highball

100 ft

H

M

N

O

spires

P
P

cliff line

steep canyonside slope

to 36, Lyons, New River Wall

Longmont reservoir

THE LION'S DEN

The Lion's Den was developed over five years ago by Lyons locals Colin Lantz and Paul Pomeroy, but remained secret until only recently. With its quiet, scenic location high above the North St. Vrain River and scattering of good granite boulders, the "Den" offers a unique getaway for boulderers burned out on the Front Range's more traveled areas. Expect crimpy problems on good, crystalline granite and mortifying highballs, as well as fun moderates with soft, pine-needle landings. Though the area isn't vast it does offer potential for new lines. Expect some lichen and loose holds. The Den is best visited in the fall or spring, as the exposed position of the boulders leaves them open to gusty winter winds and sweltering summer heat.

Directions: From the town of Lyons head west for 4.0 miles on US 36 towards Estes Park from the light at the junction of Highway 7. Turn left at the Shelly Cottages onto County Road 80, which is signed for the Longmont Dam. Follow the dirt road 2.8 miles to its end and park below the white gate.

Pass through the gate and continue west on the dirt road about 7-10 minutes (0.5 miles), passing the River Wall and Button Rock Reservoir en route. Just above the point where the stream flows into the Reservoir notice a set of power lines that cross from the south side of the stream to the north side, then back again. Where the power lines cross back again find a faint track on the left, paralleling the road and heading up into the trees. This is an old original portion of the Sleepy Lion Trail (not to be confused with the marked trailhead for the new Sleepy Lion Trail, another 0.5 miles up the road).

Follow the trail up the steep hill past six well-defined switchbacks (home of the Switchback Boulders). The Paulaner Wall is just east of the fourth switchback (it has steps) on the hillside. The Prow is about 50 yards southeast and uphill from the sixth switchback, forming a northwest-facing mini-cliff with a large ponderosa in front of it.

The trail then levels out and heads southwest through a clearing to an excellent vista point, affording views of the valley below and the high peaks to the west. From here, cut left (eastish) onto an old ranching road and follow it 200 yards into a large clearing. The rock pile atop the hill to the east is the Lion's Den Proper. Total approach time: 30-35 minutes.

To reach the Lower Den walk east from the Lion's Den Proper until you encounter an old road leading north through the woods. The Caterwaul Grotto is roughly 100 yards north and downhill along this road and sits on the canyon rim.

SWITCHBACK BOULDERS

These boulders offer an esoteric and highball venue on the steep hillside below the Lion's Den Proper. You can warm-up down here, but I wouldn't recommend it. Best visited once you're in "send mode." Don't forget your crash pad ...

A. PAULANER WALL

So named because the problems were all put up with the help of three bottles of this fine lager by one who shall remain nameless ... Expect slightly licheny problems on stone ranging from unapologetic choss to good, varnished granite. (Note: Problems #1 and #2 are on the east of the two fins of rock)

1. Lager V2 *

Climb the red face, moving left around the arete when convenient. Needs traffic.

2. Pilsner V0

Follow the dirty, right-trending crack to a blocky top-out. Jingus.

3. Hefe V3 **

Climb the slabby face via the thin horizontals. Appealing stone and continuous, thin moves.

4. Weizen V4 *

Climb the right-leaning arete where the slab meets the overhang. Thin, friable, and strangely unnerving.

B. THE PROW

A trio of hard, stellar highballs make this isolated wall well worth the short, steep slog off the trail—if you fail to send, at least you can gawk at the awe-inspiring undone line up the clean, nubbin-studded vertical face. Bring lots of crash pads, cuz these problems are high!

1. Poop Deck V0 **

Layback up the crack in the corner, moving left to finish.

2. Project V? ***

In the words of Colin Lantz, "Way highball—so thin, so high, so aesthetically perfect." The Braille trail on the vertical wall right of the corner.

3. Walk the Gangplank V7 ***

Quite serious. Climb the nose feature just right of the Braille bumps, aiming for a rounded horn at mid-height.

4. The Ice Lock V7 ** 🕐

Climb the sharp, incut seams up the orange patina on the hanging bulge feature, moving right into #5 to finish. The hard start, low and left, has yet to be freed.

5. Hoosh Pot V4 * 🕐

Start as low as possible in the crack/fin feature and climb up to the bonsai tree, taking care not to use the large loose block by the tree. V1 from a high start.

6. Blubber V0

Also the downclimb. The easy corner out right.

LION'S DEN PROPER

Though there are a handful of good outlying blocks in the trees both above and below the main area, the highest concentration of problems is found at the Den Proper, a dense maze of walls and blocks capping a scenic hillside. Problems tend toward the crimpy, so ration your skin wisely. The high, committing problems on the Big Cat Block are hard to beat, as are the strange but steep Hyperion Proboscis and the excellent Egg Boulder.

C. HYPERION PROBOSCIS

This lone block sits about 100 feet downhill and slightly northwest from The Egg on a sunny bench at the edge of the meadow, and is easily recognized by its phallic form, which points north for some odd reason—maybe a hard-on for Fo Co?

1. Hyperion Proboscis V7 ***

Sds on a good jug/flake to the right then pimp your way up the double aretes. Thuggy and unique; not for homophobes.

D. GREG'S DADA

A short but fun wall 15 feet north of the Beh Slab.

1. Greg's Dada V2 *

Up the seam/finger crack on the west-facing wall.

E. BEH SLAB

Tucked in a notch just ten feet north of The Egg, this splitter blob of granite offers kind stone that recalls the texture of the Buttermilks in Bishop, California. The rock is exceptionally featured and solid, but the landings are bad to non-existent.

1. Unknown V3 *

An interesting line up the scoops and edges on the tall northwest side of the boulder, over an interestingly uneven landing.

2. The Mariacher Factor V3 ***

Climb the west arete up to good horns. Buttermilkian.

3. The Beh Slab V0 **

Follow the flake up and right into the scoop, step left to finish.

4. Inside Moves V2 *

Start on #3 but move right from the scoop to climb the arete on porcelain flakes.

F. THE EGG

This aptly named chunk of granite is perched just west of The Corridor and just south of The Big Cat on a flat, pleasant bench. It offers good problems up crisp edges on very bulgy stone.

1. Egg Roof V7 *

Sds in a finger seam in the small cave on the northeast side of the rock. Slap up for crystals, then thrutch over as best you can. Fugly.

2. Over Easy V8 **

Start under the faint prow on the west face on a good jug. Crimps gain a tiny right-hand crystal, and a slap left to finish takes you out over the bad landing.

3. Poached V4 **

Start on #2 but move right along the horizontal to a white-stained jug, then head straight up on tiny dinner plates.

4. Scrambled V4 *

Start up and right on the high terrace, matched in a good horizontal. Crank up the face on flat crimpers to a juggy finish.

Beh Slab

The Egg

G. THE CORRIDOR

This tall but solid wall offers a few good problems on funky jugs and dinner plates like those found at City of Rocks, Idaho. It sits uphill and west of The Egg about 40 feet and the problems face south, making this a nice place to catch morning sun and stretch out your fingers. Good landings abound.

1. Schwank V1 *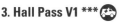

Climb the right side of the diamond-shaped block under the small roof, then stretch up over the roof for an incut bucket and finish out.

2. Linoleum V2 **

This proud line takes the scoop up the middle of the wall, heading for a faint seam to top out. V3 if you off-route the jug on the right.

3. Hall Pass V1 ***

Face climbing at its finest. Start low in the layback crack in the good tan rock, then punch straight up the wall on bizarre, wavy stone.

4. Late Bell V2

The slightly loose problem on flake holds just left of the eastern arete.

5. Main Line V1

Climb the right-trending layback on the block directly behind #3. Awkward and unpleasant.

H. HYPERION ARETE

Not to be confused with the Hyperion Proboscis, this funky little block offers a short but technical arete. It looks like a piece of bread sticking up out of the ground and sits just west of the Warm-up Block.

1. Hyperion Lunge V-Stupid

Run and jump up the center of the face, latching the grainy jugs at the lip.

2. Hyperion Arete V3 *

The short, slabby arete on the right side of the face. Start low for full value. Tricky.

I. Warm-up Block

Though quite lowball, this little fin offers a handful of cruiser problems with perfect landings. Use caution topping out. This is a useful place to start climbing due to its central location and ease of access to the other rocks, as well as a safe place to get used to the Lion's Den variety of granite.

1. South Arete V0+ *
Climb incuts and dinner plates up the rounded south arete, aiming for a small seam at the top.

2. PW Traverse V4 *
Start on #1 and cross the rock rightwards, staying low and finishing out on #5. Crimpy.

3. Moss Boss V1 *
Start on a chest-high horn and go either straight up or move right to a crimp then up to good dinner plates. Fun.

4. Choss Boss V0-
The easy hand crack splitting the east face.

5. Crack 'n Up V1 *
This line takes the short finger crack in the black rock four feet right of #3.

6. Slab Master V1
Climb the layback seam in the pink rock from a sds, off-routing the finger crack to your left. Miniature.

J. The Tooth

This is the block/wall in the corridor just west of, and behind, the Warm-up Block. A pair of good moderates grace the slightly grainy stone.

1. Rollerball V0
Climb the rampy, south-facing arete on ball-bearing slopers.

2. Canines V2 *
Start on a layback at chest height then reef up to good incuts on the rounded arete feature with the bright green lichen. Fun and aesthetic.

K. Big Cat Block

The highest, cleanest, and most aesthetic wall at Lion's Den, this exemplary chunk of stonker granite is also home to the area's scariest highballs, many of which top out at over 20 feet, sometimes over rocky landings. Expect crimpy and technical problems on immaculate, varnished stone.

West Face and Southwest Arete

1. Scaredy Cat V3 *
This terrifying line takes the finger seam/layback on the left side of the west face, topping out at a tiny tree. Insecure.

2. The Big Cat V4 ****
The best problem at the Den. Climb the layback flake/finger seam directly over the good landing, heading for a water groove up high. Classic.

3. Le Samet Corner V4 **
A real ankle-breaker. Climb the left-facing corner just right of #2. The crux comes high over the rocky landing.

4. Lion Bitch V6 **
Slap your way up the double-arete/prow via the good brown-red stone. Crimpy and technical.

Mike Freischlag on The Big Cat   photo: Matt Samet

55

5. Knee Bar Pussy V6 ** 🚗 🤚
Climb the southwest arete of the wall, moving right into #6 to finish.

LOWER SOUTH FACE

6. Punch the Kitty V5 * 🚗 🤚
Climb into the scoop on the south face then exit via tiny crimpers.

UPPER SOUTH FACE

7. Alley Cat V0+ * 🚗 🤚
The leftmost line on the upper part of the south face. Climb the clean corner into the white-stained crack. High and spooky.

8. Tigger V0+ ** 🚗 🤚
Climb the middle of the dinner-plate-covered wall directly under the pine tree.

9. Catfish V0+ * 🚗
Climb the left side of the eastern arete, moving left up high to finish in a positive layback crack in the black rock.

10. Cat Scratch Fever V2 ** 🚗 🤚
This scary line takes the eastern arete to the black bulge, then moves right onto the bulge to finish out over the horrible landing.

L. SOLITARY SPIRIT
This is a tomato-shaped blob in the forest down and diagonally right (northwest) 50 yards from the Hyperion Proboscis. This boulder is small but aesthetic in a "Font" sort of way; it's probably a bad idea to come here at the end of the day as the holds are tinous and sharp.

1. Solitary Confinement V2 *
The rounded east arete of the boulder.

2. Solitary Spirit V3 **
Harder if you're short. The aesthetic, scooped face via distant holds.

3. Seldom Seen V1 *
A decent slab/mantle problem on the west face of the boulder.

THE LOWER DEN

This grouping of boulders has lots of hidden gems—if you have the patience to find them. Expect nicely textured granite and good, pine needle landings in a forested setting (Though a few problems in the Caterwaul Grotto have uneven, rocky landings). It's generally cooler down here than up at the Den Proper, as the cavey clustering of the boulders and a cool breeze off the Continental Divide keep temperatures down.

M. HAMBURGER

This rock sits 100 feet east of Lion's Den Proper, just across and down from an old logging road leading north to the edge of the canyon. It is an elongated, northwest-facing wall with a bulge on each end.

1. Happy Meal V3

More like Unhappy Meal. Start in the horizontal crack and crank the awkward bulge on the left.

2. Hamburger V5 *

Start on a good waist-high horizontal and punch out the bulge on crimps. The direct top-out gives full, awkward V5 glory, while bailing right subtracts an entire V-grade!

N. CHEESEBURGER

This is a unique little boulder, with slopers and "eyebrow" features, 100 feet northeast of Hamburger across a grassy clearing. It offers excellent moderates over perfect landings, and hey, it really does look like a cheeseburger!

1. Supersize It V1 *

Out the crisp horizontals on the northwest face, just left of the tree. Fun.

2. Cheeseburger V3 **

Send the slopey horizontals just right of the aforementioned tree to a "Font-style" top-out.

3. Extra Cheese V3 *

The direct southwest face, aiming for a pink "smiley-face" hold with your right hand and off-routing the ledge out right. V4 ** if you low traverse into it from as far right as possible.

4. Tom's Tavern V1
Sds and climb the squatty, grotty prow via crumbling jugs.

O. THE BONEYARD

This odd west-facing wall, just visible from The Cheeseburger, is 50 feet down and to the east in a stealthy grotto behind a large spruce tree.

1. Crackyard V0- *
Climb the pleasant, arching crack on the left side of the wall.

2. Kevin's Arete V2 *
Climb the pinkish arete between the two crack lines. Phunkee!

3. The Boneyard V3 **
Sds on locks and layaways and voyage up the funky crack above. Big hands and dirty jams take you over the lip.

4. Contrived Pile V4
The face right of the crack, off-routing the crack for some strange reason.

P. CATERWAUL GROTTO

To enter the grotto, follow the road down to the canyon rim and duck right into a corridor with a small pine tree. This is a nice place to get out of the sun or the wind, with a couple of classics to boot. Though many of the landings are good, a few problems climb directly over ugly blocks. Bring plenty of pads.

CORRIDOR PROBLEMS
First two problems not pictured.

1. Sprayspot V3 *
The water groove, crisscrossed by horizontals, on the right wall of the corridor across from #2.

2. Sprayflake V2
Five feet right of #3. Start on a horn hold in the horizontal then make a long reach over the bulge, eventually joining the chossy flake.

3. The Howling V4 **
The black-colored left wall of the corridor, behind the pine tree. Stretch to a jug than make your way up the wall as best you can …

4. Ichiban V4 **
Start matched in the dirty (but juggy) horizontal then move up into underclings then back left along the lip of the roof.

LOWER PROBLEMS
(on the same boulder as The Howling but wrapping left and north downhill):

5. Sweetness V0 *
A fun jug haul—sds on the good lip and move past the huecos.

6. Right Now V4 ***
A great highball! Continuous crimping on the tall black face above the evil, rampy landing.

7. Wrong Now V1
The ultra-licheny groove/nose below #6. Good landing, needs travel.

8. Sickness V4 *
So utterly sick! Up the slabby red face via thin, sharp holds to gain the water scoops and a dirty top-out.

9. Steadman's Heffer V2 *
This problem is on the small buttress out right and features a perfect, sandy landing.

Q. COUGAR CACHE WALL
This wall can be hard to locate, but it's worth the effort. It features varnished stone with a red patina and user-friendly, wind-sculpted holds. Head west 70 feet from Caterwaul Grotto to get here. The wall faces north and commands an excellent view of the valley. Many link-ups and variations are possible on this highly-featured gem.

1. Cougar Left V1 *
The leftmost line on the wall via positive holds.

2. Bathtubs V0+ **
A monster-fun jug haul. Sds off the landing block and work left three feet, then cruise back right into the bathtubs and up.

Naomi Guy on the Cougar Cache Wall   photo: Matt Samet

3. Cougar's Crank V1 **

Sds from the right side of the landing block then move straight up the wall on incuts to the funky little horn. V2 ** if you traverse in from the right on the diagonaling crack.

4. Cougar'n'a'bing'bing, Bling! V3 **

From the undercling flake head straight up the bomber, red wall on small edges, off-routing the bathtub out right.

5. Cougar Cooze V1 *

Start about three feet right of #4. Head for the diagonaling bathtub, then scunge your way over the lip.

6. Cougar Cache Traverse V3 **

Like many a climber in the Boulder area, this fine traverse goes both ways.

FLATIRONS

Elizabeth Culbertson on Highlander   photo: Fred Knapp

THE FLATIRONS

Like hiking? Like wandering around lost in ivy-filled gullies, cursing the guidebook authors who so earnestly tried to help you find their newest cache of hidden Fountain boulders? Then the Flatirons are for you! Many lifetime's worth of undiscovered blocks await the hearty in the peaceful Boulder Mountains, where thick pine forests and talus-filled gullies blend into the background of ubiquitous maroon slabs rearing up above Boulder. However, recent discoveries like the Terrain Boulders, the Blues Boulders, the Upper Satellite Boulders and the Green Mountain Boulders—all excellent clusters of varied Fountain sandstone—should keep you plenty occupied if you don't feel like casting off on your own.

The rock in the Flatirons ranges from the downright brilliant (varnished maroon stone with vibrant green lichen streaks and a plethora of solid pockets, huecos and crimpers) to the abominable (chossy white or reddish stone that resembles kitty litter). With the thousands of boulders and bouldering possibilities that dot the landscape, it's up to you to figure out which is which. Good luck and happy bouldering!

ECO-NOTE: The Flatirons are being over-run by a non-indigenous plant called Hound's Tongue, which produces scads of small, circular brown burrs (these love to attach themselves to your clothing). When removing these burrs, please dispose of them in a small plastic baggie instead of tossing them on the ground, thus preventing the spread of this noxious plant.

THIRD FLATIRON

This area includes the already described Ghetto (see Colorado Bouldering) as well as the handful of good blocks that have been found within a half-mile radius of Boulder's best-known landmark.

HOUSE PARTY BOULDER

This enormous chunk of solid, featured Fountain Sandstone high on the east face of Green Mountain (directly behind the summit of the Third Flatiron) is a great, out-of-the-way venue for highball and traverse aficionados. The long (65-foot) traverse of the north and west faces of the boulder is an ultra-classic voyage on fluted sandstone reminiscent of the Red River Gorge.

Directions: From the Bluebell Shelter hike 10-15 minutes up the road. Then follow the Third Flatiron Trail, which branches right off the Royal Arch Trail about five minutes up. Walk another 15-20 minutes, passing the Lower Satellite Boulders and emerging onto a large talus field below the north face of the Third. A trail leads uphill (west) from the middle of this talus field and is signed with "3rd Flatiron Descent Trail." Follow this steep, rugged trail uphill another 10-15 minutes until it hits the ridge behind the Third's summit. The north face of the boulder is right on the trail. Approach time: 40-50 minutes.

1. Sod It! V3 *
This 30-foot high problem is a three-star problem buried under two star's worth of lichen. Start just right of the northeast arete and climb the scooped, slabby wall above.

2. Traverse V6 ***
Traversing doesn't really get any better than this. Start below #1 and punch right, eventually turning the northwest arete of the boulder to finish low across huecos and pods at the lip of a roof.

3. Scenic Traverse V1 **
On the upper tier of the west face, just above the finish to the traverse, find this huecoed wall. Go right to left. A fall off this one would be ugly.

4. House Party V2 ***
Start on edges near the left (west) end of the huge southern chasm and fire up for a ledge. Reach high for another horizontal then crimp your way through the crux exit moves, 25 feet above a blocky pit. Aesthetic.

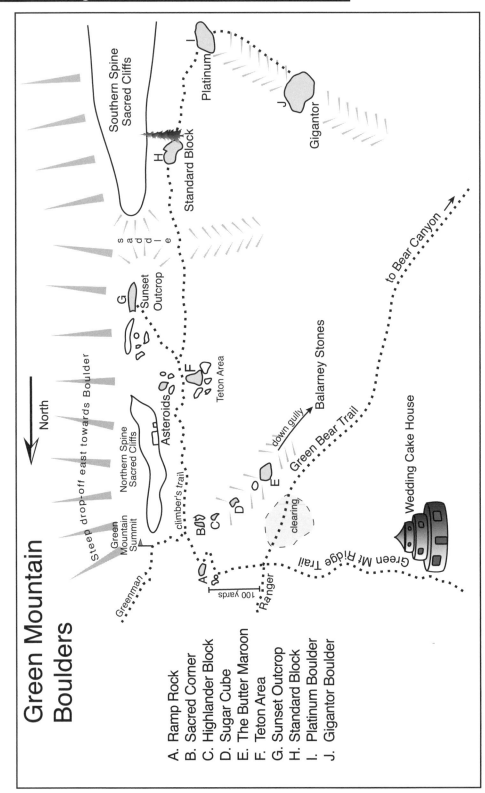

Green Mountain Boulders

A. Ramp Rock
B. Sacred Corner
C. Highlander Block
D. Sugar Cube
E. The Butter Maroon
F. Teton Area
G. Sunset Outcrop
H. Standard Block
I. Platinum Boulder
J. Gigantor Boulder

GREEN MOUNTAIN BOULDERS

This extensive area with lots of completed problems on good stone and plenty of potential lies on the peaceful west side of Green Mountain, facing away from the heinous froo-fraa of yuppie-packed Boulder. Though the blocks are somewhat scattered and hard to find due to the thick pine forest blanketing the mountain's slopes, many of them sit in convenient fall-lines in the gullies below the Sacred Cliffs.

The ambience is unbeatable: forests, meadows, and unimpeded views of the striking Indian Peaks to the west. Seasonal bird closures (Feb 1- July 31) at the Sacred Cliffs block access to many of the boulders higher on the ridge. Here's a tip: Respect all closure signs and call Boulder Mountain Parks (303-441-3408) if you're unsure as to where you can or can't climb during the closure.

Expect much walking and exploration, as it is difficult to readily locate many of the boulders your first time out. Better yet, have someone give you the tour or consult Bob Horan's exhaustive guidebook: Best of Boulder Bouldering, Falcon Press, 2000. The vast majority of the boulders in this area were developed by Horan over the last 20 years and his guidebook provides explicit directions to all of the boulders.

Directions: From the intersection of Broadway and Baseline in Boulder drive 6.1 miles west up Baseline (soon Flagstaff) road, reaching a shoulder where the road flattens out after the last hairpin turn on the ascent. Park in a pullout on the right and head for the Green Mountain West Ridge trailhead on the south side of the road. This trail follows the expansive ridge west for about a mile to the summit of Green Mountain, coming to a four-way intersection (at 20-25 minutes) with the Ranger Trail and the Green-Bear Trail (well below the summit pyramid).

Green Mountain North: While all the boulders on this section of the mountain sit more or less in the same gully, there are two different approaches for the upper and lower areas.

For the upper area (Ramp Rock, The Sacred Corner, The Sugar Cube, The Highlander Block) stay on the Green Mountain West Ridge Trail heading east from the intersection, reaching Ramp Rock after five very steep minutes of hiking. The other boulders are slighly south and down from here.

For the lower area (The Butter Maroon) follow the Green-Bear Trail downhill and south for about five minutes from the intersection, crossing a large open area before hitting a ridge. Immediately upon hitting the ridge drop left into the grassy gully (the northernmost fall-line from the Sacred Cliffs) to find the boulder. Alternately, drop 50 yards straight down the gully from The Sugar Cube to reach the Butter Maroon.

Green Mountain South: The bulk of the bouldering sits below the southern spine of the Sacred Cliffs. Continue east on the Green Mountain West Ridge Trail past a couple of switchbacks until you reach the obvious Ramp Rock, a green slab with multiple overlaps right on the trail. A faintly-marked game trail takes off 150 feet south of here, just past a "Closed for revegetation" sign and a pile of logs. Avoid the closed area by hiking high or low to pick up the trail further along. Do your best to stay on the trail and tread lightly.

Gigantor Boulder

This trail then winds its way south, passing numerous areas (such as the impressive Teton, a gigantic pyramid-shaped boulder west of the trail and surrounded by many other worthy boulders) on its way to the Standard Block.

The Standard Block sits just south and west of the sandy saddle between the two spines of the Sacred Cliffs, about ten minutes off the Green Mountain trail. The Platinum Block is six minutes further south and sits about 60 yards downhill from the prominent box-car shaped cliff on the northern tip of the Southern Spine of the Sacred Cliffs. The Gigantor Boulder is obscured by trees in the big gully down and vaguely west-northwest from here, about five minutes away.

Areas have been developed further south and west of here. Please be aware that this is a sensitive erosion-prone area that might be better left unvisited.

GREEN MOUNTAIN NORTH

If your bandy little legs are quaking by the time you reach the four-way intersection then you may want to stop and boulder here, as the areas further south require a bit more slogging. Though most of the rocks are a ways off the trail, use discretion and mind your P's and Q's while bouldering here. The Butter Maroon is one of the finest sandstone blocks in the Boulder area, while the other boulders offer a host of good problems on varied, solid rock.

A. RAMP ROCK

This slabby, green wall just off the trail provides a good warm-up and a useful landmark for finding the game trail, a faint track which takes you to the southerly areas. Ramp Rock sits five minutes up the Green Mountain West Ridge Trail from the four-way intersection below.

1. West Slab V0-V1 *

Many variations possible. The most obvious line moves right to left along the undercling flake and tops out in the groove on the left.

B. SACRED CORNER

With decent landings and a handful of fun moderates on Flagstaff-like, pebbled stone, this little grotto just off the trail is a great place to warm up. From Ramp Rock walk 150 feet south on the main trail, then follow the faint trail another 80 feet south, passing a seasonal closure sign. Drop 20 feet west down the steep slope into this south-facing alcove.

NORTHERN FIN

1. Riff-Raff V3 *
Climb the center of the south face of the alcove's northern fin via diagonaling edges.

2. Love Triangles V1
Seven feet right of #1, layback the offwidth then lean left into the groove system.

3. Sinister V2
Layback up the left side of the offwidth. Easier if you use holds back in the crack.

4. Karen's Crack V0-
The cruiser hand crack in the back (east) end of the alcove. No chimneying!

SOUTHERN FIN

5. Pathological Arete V0+ *
This problem is on the north face of the alcove's southern fin. Climb the shady red wall via a right-trending flake system which leads you to the arete.

6. Cola V1 *
The fun excursion climbs the west side of the arete around from #5. Start on a small seam studded with large crystals and move left to the arete to finish.

7. Peppy Slab V3 **
Start on the good crystals on #6 but stay right, climbing into the faint black streak on tiny pebbles to finish.

8. Addictive V3 *
Start six feet right of #6 and climb straight into the scoop above. Shares some holds with #7.

9. Princess of Darkness V1
The pleasant line on incut pebbles up the south face, just uphill from the arete.

10. Three Strikes V0
Master the center of the south face via the ramp and good holds above it.

C. HIGHLANDER BLOCK

This appealing cube of sandstone sits due west and downhill 100 feet from Sacred Corner. It has a distinctive northwest face, which sports two high, clean aretes.

1. Northeast Flakes V0+ *
Sds on good flakes, then traverse up and left along the flake system on killer jugs.

2. Highlander V2 **
Start above the embedded block then move past crimps to the left-trending flake, which you follow up and left to the lip near the left arete.

3. Highlander Arete V3 **
A slightly gripping excursion up the right arete of the wall. Fortunately the crux comes at mid-height, before the mossy top-out.

D. THE SUGAR CUBE

Yee-haw! A smaller replica of the Butter Maroon with fewer problems, this unique blob of solid, overhanging maroon stone in a quiet meadow is well worth a visit. Walk downhill and west 50 yards from the Highlander Block, passing through a pine grove littered with smallish boulders that offer congenial problems in the V0-V1 range.

1. Middleman V4 **

Long moves to hidden incuts define this powerful line, which starts on a good left-facing layback towards the right side of the west face.

2. The Flying Overhang V3 ***

The obvious line up the flake system on the arete. Save some gumption for the awkward, thrutchy top-out.

3. Mat Mover V1

This uninspiring line is located just behind the tree on the right side of the south face.

E. THE BUTTER MAROON

This dreamy boulder sits in a nice, grassy gully just off the Green-Bear Trail and offers a handful of stellar highballs in the middle V-grades. Expect engaging moves on colorful, swirly rock featuring sharpish crimpers. Nearby boulders worth checking out, but not described here, include the Power Boulder (a little ways uphill) and Walrus Boulder (50 yards down gully). They both offer thin climbing on bulging stone.

1. Land O' Boulders V4 **

This sustained, crimpy line climbs into a small, right-facing corner on the left side of the northwest face. Much harder from a sds.

2. Sweet Arete V5 ****

A perfect line up the nose of the boulder, finishing in a funky finger crack feature. An eliminate, Peregrine V7, climbs the seams on the left sans the arete.

3. Buffalo Gold V4 ***

Oh yeah, baby! Climb the flake feature just right of the arete to a puzzling top-out.

4. Parkay V5 ***

Looks to be much harder. Climb the proud black streak right of the flake.

5. Butter Rum V3

An also-ran. Climb friable flakes into a bathtub jug by the small tree. Some holds have broken.

Green Mountain South

With a remote feel and beautiful views both to the east and west, the boulders south of Green Mountain's summit make for a rewardingly obscure experience. Both spines of the Sacred Cliffs offer a labyrinth of walls and boulders along the summit ridge, with many interesting blocks hidden in the trees down below. Take your time, explore, and tread lightly. This is a beautiful, seldom-visited zone which we should do our best to keep pristine and impact-free.

F. The Teton Area

This is the next good concentration of blocks south of Sacred Corner. Walk south along the Maroon Trail for five minutes past Sacred Corner, passing along the base of the Northern Spine of the Sacred Cliffs and many other bouldering possibilities. The Teton itself is hard to miss—it's a 30- to 50-foot-tall, crystal-studded pyramid poking out of a jumble of blocks just west of the game trail.

The Teton

When does a highball become a solo? Sample the tall, committing lines up small crystals on this one-of-a-kind spire and you'll soon find out. Use caution with the more protruding pebbles and crystals— they have been known to break!

1. Mangy Moose V3 *
A huge dead tree leans against the ride side of the west face. Start left of this and climb the steep, pebbly groove then amble left up the high, crystal-studded slab to the summit (5.7).

2. Grande V2 ***
Start from the good-landing tier under the southeast face and climb the sustained wall via tiny nubbins and crystals. Pretty damn cool …

3. Tits Ville V0
Also the downclimb. The grotty yet obvious crack/flare line up the east face.

4. The Hostel V3 *
Climb the slabby northeast arete of the boulder, moving slightly right at the finishing bulge to top out at a hangerless bolt. Dirty.

The Asteroids and Other Boulders

This is the pleasant grouping of boulders surrounding the Teton on its north and east sides. These varied rocks offer good moderates as well as a few thin desperates on some of the steeper walls. Some problems are still crumbly, but this area should clean up well with traffic.

G. SUNSET OUTCROP

This radically overhanging west-facing wall makes a useful landmark for finding other blocks in the area and provides breathtaking views to the east and the west. It sits at the southern tip of the Northern Spine of the Sacred Cliffs on the northern end of the open, gravelly saddle between the two Spines. Plenty of existing problems and potential desperates grace the walls and boulders just north of here along the ridge.

1. Aretes Away V2 **

The thuggy, scenic arete on the far left side of the wall.

2. Cracking Up V2 **

This is the overhanging crack just right of the arete. The top-out is awkward.

3. Crystal Dyno V8 ***

A difficult line near the center of the wall, starting on a large, white crystal and cranking sick moves to the lip.

4. Sunscreen V1

The somewhat uninspiring little line on the right side of the wall.

H. STANDARD BLOCK

With four splitter lines on its multicolored, highball south face, this exemplary block personi-fies what all other choss in the Flatirons aspires—yet fails—to be. Killer views of Walker Ranch and the Indian Peaks sweeten the deal. The block sits just below the cliff line on the northern end of the Southern Spine.

1. Wavey V2 ** 🌀

The highball southwest arete. Climb vertical slots and pinches to a slightly grubby top-out.

2. The Groove V3 ****

The superlative central line up huecos in the tan streak.

3. Standard Shield V2 **

Layback on dishes in the maroon streak, heading for a good hueco in the maroon-colored rib.

4. Crystal Scoop V4 ***

Sds on the east end of the south face and climb the orange-streaked scoop via small but positive crystals. Kinaesthetically pleasing.

5. Crystal Arete V3 *

Sds as for #4 but crank right around the arete and head up to good holds. V0 from the stand-up.

6. Short Crystal V0

The downclimb. Start on jugs at chest height in the middle of the east face and climb the cobbles.

Josh Deuto spotted by Pete Zoller on Socrate's Overhang

I. Platinum Boulder

Steep, remote and punishing. The long, overhanging west/southwest wall of this boulder offers a number of killer overhangs on positive holds reminiscent of Hueco Tanks. A couple of undone lines promise to be very hard. Near-perfect landings more than make up for the flakiness of a few holds.

1. Plato's Arete V7 ***

Sds with your hands on good horizontal holds at chest height then move left to the severely overhanging arete. Superb.

2. Socrate's Overhang V5 ***

Start on #1 but trend right on small incuts to a horn at the lip. Powerful and crimpy.

3. Pop Overhangs V3 *

Throw from a horn at arm's reach to the juggy lip 13 feet right of #2. Finish via a "classic" mantle.

4. Main Hang V7 **

Big moves out a big roof. Start on the incut and move left, eventually throwing for a slopey cobble high and left at the lip.

5. Platinum Overhang V8 ***

Harder since holds have broken? The incredible line leading out the steep-ass maroon face to a shaky-looking horn/flake below the lip.

J. Gigantor Boulder

One of largest single boulders in the Flatirons, this hidden behemoth doesn't reveal its true size until you stumble onto it amidst a thick grove of trees. Aaah, if only we could still bolt ... Anyway, an interesting 5.12 lead out the big roof and a pair of proud highballs on the south face make this boulder worth a visit.

1. Tobar V7

Harder since holds have broken. Climb the heinous-sick looking line on the left side of the bulging alcove on the south face.

2. The Surf V6 **

Big, bad, bold and butch. Punch your way straight out the alcove via layaways and sloping edges. A jug flake at mid-height lets you either psyche up for the dicey exit in the bowl out left or cop out and jump to the pads.

Pete Zoller surfing

Rocky Balboas / Upper Satellites

The Satellite boulderfields lie to the south of the Second Flatiron and encompass two distinct areas. The lower area is described in Colorado Bouldering. The Rocky Balboas are a short, albeit strenuous, five-minute hike uphill. Lines in The Rockies are good quality and often entail tall slabs, or else short power problems. If the lower Satellite boulders are not to your liking, or are crowded, The Rockies are a quiet change.

Directions:
From Chatauqua Park walk south up the old paved road (Bluebell Road) that begins behind the ranger station. Continue on the road past the Bluebell Shelter and take the trail for the Second and Third Flatirons (follow signs) over a talus slope to the split of the two trails. Continue on the Third Flatiron Trail past the BBC Boulder and lower Satellites (chalk is present year round). Walk up the trail another five minutes then head north to the Second Flatiron (do not hike past the western edge of the Third Flatiron). The boulders are found near the drainages on the south side of the Second.

Wildlife Closure Area The Flatirons have a seasonal closure for raptor nesting from February 1 to July 31st. Please stay away from the closed areas.

Boom Boulder

A large block on the southern edge of the Rocky Balboas. A lichen-covered dihedral is on the north face.

1. Boom V6 **
Climb up the north face just left of the left-facing dihedral. This problem sees little traffic—expect a mossy finish.

2. V2 *
Climb the edge problem on the far right side of the north face. Bad landing on uneven blocks.

3. V0 * (not pictured)
Climb the south face slab.

4. V3 * (not pictured)
Climb the southeast arete. Harder slab problems are just to the right of the arete.

East End Block

This block is found 25 feet northeast from Boom Boulder. A slightly overhanging triangular-shaped south face defines the block.

1. V0 * (not pictured)
Climb the juggy west face.

2. V4 **
Climb the sloping ramps on the south face to gain the left arete and a tenuous finish. Variants are spread across the face.

DA BOULDER

Next to the East End Block to the west. A short steep arete left of a huge pine defines the block.

1. V4 *

Climb out of the steep wall on the southwest face.

2. V5 **

From a low start climb out the south arete. A very good problem on tasty rock.

3. V0 *

Climb any of the slab problems (all V0) on the south face by the pine tree.

Da Boulder

TRIVIAL BOULDER

Uphill 25 yards to the west from Boom is a short block (10') with easy V0s.

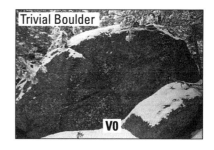
Trivial Boulder

LICHEN BLOCK

A tall boulder lit up by fluorescent lichen on the south face. The block is located 25 yards west and uphill from Boom behind a couple of pines. Spitting distance to the north from Trivial Block.

V3 **

Climb the colorful south face on good edges and long reaches.

Lichen Block

THE MORTIMERIZER V1 **

Just south from Trivial Boulder, and above Boom, is a double arete problem at the Wildlife Closure Area signs.

The Mortimerizer

ADDITIONAL BOULDERS:

These two boulders are found in the drainage between the Upper and Lower Satellites.

HARD ARETE V?

Climb the steep southeast arete from a low start and finish up the slab or traverse right for bonus pump.

HOBO BOULDER

This distinct boulder is downhill from the arete to the north (approximately 60 yards) and sits next to the Second Flatiron. The selection of (somewhat contrived) problems range from V2 to V6 and face east (down the drainage).

VERTICAL BOULDER

Problems on this gorgeous east face range from the easiest on the far left to excruciatingly thin problems on the right.

Miah Jones on Hobo   photo: Jay Droeger

GROSS RESERVOIR

Pete Zoller attempting Singular Objective   photo: Phillip Benningfield

GROSS RESERVOIR

The best bouldering area by a dam site near Boulder. Opinions on this area vary, but the rock is solid granite well above the sweltering plains. Four different zones constitute the Gross experience. Differences are stark: the oldest and newest developed areas are located in a fire destruction zone, another is next to a fly-fishing stream; the third by railroad tracks. Whichever area you visit be assured the challenges are substantial with sick problems up to V12.

Directions: From Boulder drive up Baseline Road to Flagstaff Mountain. Continue 8.9 miles from the base of Flagstaff over the summit and past Walker Ranch to Gross Dam Road. Take a left on Gross Dam Road (a dirt road).

Hazard County, the newest area developed at Gross Reservoir, is located at The Burn at a left-turning hairpin turn at mile 0.8. There is currently parking for several cars and a cairned trail leading to the boulders.

The Burn is located at 0.8 and 1.2 miles down the Gross Dam Road. Parking is on the right at 0.9 and 1.1 miles. Further directions are found in the text with The Burn.

The Damnation Boulders parking is located at 2.3 miles down road. Park on the left directly before the guardrail and hairpin turn. A trail leads behind the guardrail to a dirt road that goes to the dam. The boulders are located a couple hundred yards down the road on the right. If you miss them your eyes are not open!

The Freight Train parking is located 4.2 miles on the left in a large lot. Park and hop the wooden fence (do not take the Crescent Meadow Trail) and walk across the meadow to the south (a wooded hillside is on the far end of the meadow). Hit the woods and an old roadbed then go left and walk 200 yards. A small cliff band faces due south near the railroad tracks.

HAZARD COUNTY

Fairly tall boulders of the same quality as the Damnation Boulders with mostly overhanging problems make this a great winter area. This was recently developed by Kevin Murphy, Ryan Fields and other locals.

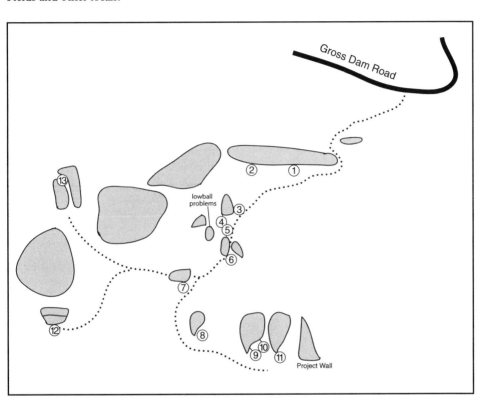

WARM-UP BLOCK

Located on the trail as one walks to the top of the cliff. Various problems exist on this block, but only one is shown on the topo.

1. Middle Line V3 ✱✱

THANKLES CLIFF

The north end of a cliff band past a pine tree where the cliff shortens to "boulder size."

1. The Shield V5 ✱✱
Thin climbing. Stay direct for the true V5 experience.

2. Thankles Traverse V4
Follow pockets to end of bulge and top out. A pad won't help the landing.

WAYLON JENNINGS BOULDER

Located 15 yards below Thankles.

3. What About Waylon? V2 *

Climb the face using broken cracks.

4. The Waylon Jennings Memorial Arete V3 ***

Left of #3

***Three lowball problems on a nearby block are good for warming up.

THE BOAR'S NEST BLOCK

Fifteen feet west of the Waylon Jennings Boulder.

5. V2 **

An excellent warm-up.

6. Boar's Nest V5 ***

A tricky sds leads to great crimps to slopers and a jug top-out.

Daisy Duke   photo: Kevin Murphy

CRAZY COOTER BLOCK

Drop down to the north 30-40 feet and look for a nice overhang above you.

7. Crazy Cooter V2 **

A sds to a left-angling crack to a reasonable top-out.

DAISY DUKE BOULDER

Drop down 50 feet to the southwest and look for an obvious boulder on the left.

8. Daisy Duke V6 ***

Start sitting with the right hand on a big slopey side-pull and left hand on a low crimp on the left arete. Excellent dyno move.

The Frangilator   photo: Kevin Murphy

GROTTO AREA

Continue south to a large grouping of boulders.

BOULDER #9

9. The Frangilator V8 ** 🔵
Slightly contrived at the start. Begin with both hands in the crack and continue through a roof utilizing knee-bars and top out straight up the arete. A knee pad is recommended.

10. Head and Shoulders V6 **
A sds to a big undercling. Look out for the Boss Hog boulder behind your head.

BOSS HOG BOULDER

11. DVY V6 * 🔵 🔵**
The obvious arete. Great slopers to a tricky crux top-out.

PROJECT WALL

Great futuristic lines. The obvious left face has seen attempts but no ascents. There is the possibility for two more lines to the right.

DEAD TREE BOULDER

Head back up to Crazy Cooter and drop down to the south looking for a fallen dead tree. Follow the tree to the boulder.

12. Scott's Dyno V3 * 🔵**
A few pads are recommended if you plan on falling.

GENERAL LEE BLOCK

Follow topo to find this block.

13. General Lee V7 * 🔵**
Start low in a slot and climb directly out. An exciting dyno leads to a slopey arete. Traverse that for 15 feet to an inobvious topout.

*** Several problems can be found on overhanging blocky rock just to the right of the exit moves on General Lee.

THE BURN

This zone has variety; there are long traverses, and gorgeous tall slabs and, sadly, chipped pockets. One idiot climber's near-sighted vision spoiled many lines by drilling over 30 holes. Luckily the destruction is contained on mostly one block. The natural lines offer a handful of entertaining problems.

THE WARM-UP TRAVERSE BOULDER

This long wall is located just before the parking at 0.9 miles. Walk back the way you came on Gross Dam Road to an Open Space boundary sign (50 yards). The boulder is visible 50 yards to the north.

Warm-up Variations V0-V4 **

A smorgasbord of problems can be done across the boulder's southeast face. A few hard mantles are on the left side with casual jug hauls from low starts in the middle.

Warm-up Traverse V5 **

From the far left side climb across the entire face to an exit on the far right.

NATURAL APPARATUS AREA (MAIN BURN ZONE)

The name is not befitting; a mindless chipper abused the rock with only his self-serving interests in sight. I could go on and on about how stupid the chipping is, but the twit who did it should feel some shame now that boulderers climb V15. The unchipped lines vary from casual slabs to a couple of super fine problems that will challenge even the bouldering metaphysical guru.

Directions: From the parking at 1.1 miles, on the right of Gross Dam Road, walk down the road past the power line pole #221. Continue 25 yards to a blocked two-car parking spot then head north (left off the road towards the big dome). The first block is 40-odd yards down a faint trail (under the powerline).

POWER BOULDER

Probably not the name the first climbers gave it—but big deal. The block is located on the south end of a boulderfield consisting of a handful of boulders. A distinct left-angling crack is on the south face.

1. V2 ** 🪨 ✋
Climb the left side of the west face starting on huge incuts to the arete and a balancy top-out.

2. V0 * 🪨
Climb up and right from the same start as #1.

3. V2 *
A traverse can be done either way on the west face.

4. V1 *
Climb the southwest arete from a stand up and finish left. A V4 can be done, starting low on the arete, to bad slopers and a thin seam, then finishing up the black face.

5. Avante Guardian V7 ***
One of the finest lines at Gross! Climb the south face bulge starting on a left-hand undercling and right-hand finger jam. Finish straight up to a hidden seam over the lip or continue left for more moves.

6. V3 *
Climb the right side of the south face, off an undercling, to bad slopers.

GREEN SLAB BLOCK
Twenty yards closer to the dome is a low-angle bulbous boulder.

1. V2 **
This one doesn't have a bad landing but you will want a spot. Climbs the west face bulge to a huge hidden hueco.

2. V0
A selection of slabby V0 lines can be done on the lichen-covered south face.

3. V0
Climb the east face just left of the pine tree.

Krong on Green Slab V2

*** Uphill from the Green Slab Block are two small boulders. The first encountered has one-move problems. The block approximately 50 yards west has a V2 on the southwest face (pictured at right). More blocks are near the dome but require serious gumption, many pads and excellent spotters.

V2

NATURAL APPARATUS BOULDER

Downhill and east a mere 25 yards from the Green Slab Block. A trail weaves through the trees.

1. V0 **

Climb the left arete on the west face. Also used as the downclimb.

2. V2 *

Climb straight up just right of #1, not using big holds until up high.

3. V0 **

Climb the middle of the west face trending right on the best holds. Also a good downclimb.

4. V3 *

A sds just right of #3 moving up to a natural pocket. Easy finish.

5. V5 *

A sds on the southwest arete. Sloping holds and a sharp crimp keep the problem from garnishing more stars.

***The first chipped problem in the area is on the south face with old bolts rusting away on the fine granite. It's not too hard to climb but a f*%#ing shame.

6. Party Trick V4 **

On the north side is a clean face with tiny crimps to a big throw and a jug. This problem attracts many suitors; it's fun to watch your friends flail and moan. A tall V0 starts the same as #6 but climbs the arete behind the pine tree.

7. V0 ***

A stunning low-angle slab on the west face. Slabs don't get more enjoyable than this.

*** A couple of sporadic V0-V1 problems are west and north on the smaller blocks 10-20 yards away.

CHIPPED BOULDER

The block is located 20 yards east of Natural Apparatus. Most lines are chipped so I have not graded them. The destruction of the boulder is the saddest accomplishment ever achieved by a nefarious climber too self-absorbed to see beyond his own petty goals. Chipped problems are not pictured or described.

1. The Conundrum V9 **

On the north face is a beautiful lichen-covered seam. Climb the seam using bizarre sequences and finish in the wide groove up and left.

2. V0
On the west face are casual V0 up-climbs and the downclimb. A butt-dragging traverse skirts the lowest flanks.

3. V4
Climb over the mini-roof just left of the seam on the southwest face to terrible pebbles.

4. V0
Climb up broken seams on the right side of the southwest face.

DAMNATION BOULDERS

The blocks in this zone are very high quality with a handful of the most aesthetic granite problems on the Front Range. The environment here offers great bouldering, good fishing and a quiet place to rip flesh from your fingers.

***Please tread lightly here as the boulders rest on a fragile hillside (stay on trails).

Pete Takeda on One Foot to Go

SOUTH SLAB BOULDER

The second block encountered from the road (the first one is too short to merit inclusion). The block has a tall south face with a diagonal seam on the right side.

1. V1 *
Climb the vertical west face.

2. One Foot to Go V4 **
Climb the seam and arete on the left side of the south face. The problem, for its moderate grade, rebuts many attempts.

3. V0
Climb the right-trending crack on the right of the south face. Another V0 is on the east face.

CLAP BLOCK

The short block 15 feet east of First Boulder. Many contrived problems can be done beyond the established problems.

1. V0
A sds on the north face off the low horizontal crack.

2. V1
A sds on the northwest arete.

The Clap

3. The Clap V3 ** 🔵

Start low on the west face off underclings. Climb straight up to a sloping lip then a good slot and belly-scraping top-out.

4. V0

A low-angle slab on the east face.

JUMP BOULDER

The large block just west of The Clap.

1. V5 *** 🔵🔵

A spectacular problem on the northeast face. Start with a big jump to the sloping shelf then move to the right-angling arete. Good holds up high but you'll still feel way off the deck!

2. V3 * 🔵

A low start just right of the crack on north face, then move left above small block.

3. V3 **

Same start as #2 but move right on good crimps to an awkward exit. A sloping problem is just right.

4. V0 🔵

Several V0 warm-ups on the west face.

POCKET BLOCK

The best damn boulder at the Damnation! Located 20 feet uphill from Jump Boulder. A couple of lines climb the pockets on this amazing boulder.

1. Feel the Bass V5 * 🔵🔵

Climb the leftmost crack above the backbreaking blocks on the south face.

2. Turn That Frown Upside Down V12 *** 🔵🔵

The yuckiest and most striking line left of Singular Objective. Climbs the shallow pockets on the left side of the pocketed overhang.

3. Singular Objective V11 ***
Climb the right line of pockets on the southeast face.
Easily one of the finest boulder problems in Colorado!

BLOCK FIVE
Just east of the Pocket Boulder.

1. V0
Wide crack on the west face.

2. V1 *
Climbs the crack on the south face. A sds low and left
then up the arete.

*** Directly east is a south-facing V1 slab and east
again, hidden in a thin slot, is a silly little V3 squeeze
problem.

BLOCK SIX (NOT PICTURED)
The lowest boulder on the south end of the
boulderfield. A tall overhanging south face defines
the boulder.

Jim Redo on Block Five's V1

1. V5 **
Sloping problem on the far-left side of the south face.

2. Poison Ivy Arete V2 **
A great problem on the east arete, with an atrocious landing. A casual V0 can be done on the
slab forming the right side of the arete.

Instant Classic V5 ** (not pictured)
A heart-shaped boulder directly above the Pocket Boulder and through the broken talus
steps. A V1 is just left.

THE SLABS (NOT PICTURED)
Located just left of Instant Classic on the long southwest-facing slab.

1. V2 **
The left slab problem climbing terribly thin edges.

2. V3 **
The slab that climbs directly above a foot ramp near the ground to a horrific top-out. The problem
isn't too high but you feel as if you will explode off the holds and land on the rocks below.

V4 **
A short north-facing overhang problem located 50 feet above the Pocket Boulder and past a
southwest face littered with slab problems (The Slabs). The boulder sits directly west of the
boulderfield's largest block, in a small passageway.

JAY'S BOULDER

A small block directly east and below the largest boulder in the field (30 feet east of Instant Classic). Two pines stand in front of the problems.

1. V0

Easy left-trending flake on the left of the block's south face. An entertaining throw to the sloping lip can be done at V3.

2. Ticky Ticky Man V6 ***

Start on low edges on right side of south face then move to the sloping arete to a hard finish (easier to top out to the left).

V2 **

Just above Jay's Boulder is a colorful east face with a problem utilizing the left arete and positive edges. Pictured at right.

V5 **

Directly above the V2 is an overhang facing east. Climb the left arete from a low start.

V2

FREIGHT TRAIN

The Train is a petite cliff band that is great to climb on in the winter. The south face offers more double-scoop problems than most boulders in the Boulder area.

***Problems are listed left to right. Only the main problems are listed (rest assured there are a few additional squeeze jobs).

1. The Prancing Cow V4 *

A sds on the cliff's left side starts off a low undercling to the seam then busts right to a flat edge and then a jug.

2. Chubby Bunny V7 ***

Start low at the base of the crystal band then move left on bad edges and a perfect left-hand pinch. A throw is next to a finger-ripping edge and reasonable top-out.

3. V2 ***

Start just right of the crystal band and climb straight up on excellent holds.

4. V3 *

Start just right of #3 then move behind the pine tree and continue up the right-trending break. Your basic terrifying boulder problem.

5. V0 ***

Start right of the pine tree and follow fantastic edges and jugs and flakes to the top.

6. V3 **

Start on right of V-slot and climb straight up. Hard after the initial bulge.

7. V2 **

Start off a rock pedestal and trend right along a diagonal break.

8. V2 ***

Start in the middle of the right bulge (eight feet right of #7), move up to a sloping shelf then the horizontal break to top out moving right.

9. V1 *

Climb the left-angling crack just right of #8.

10. The Muckler V1 * (not pictured)

Climb up the slab just right of the crack utilizing an undercling at 10 feet.

TERRAIN BOULDERS

Miah Jones wondering What About Bob?   photo: Jay Droeger

TERRAIN BOULDERS

Jay Droeger led the rediscovery of this fine cluster of blocks in the late 1990s, thus the area also bears the moniker "Droegerland." This shady hang offers one of the better concentrations of bouldering in the Flatirons (meaning, once you drop your pad you don't have to hike another mile to get to the next boulder, as is often the case up here). The boulders are well protected from the elements by a dense forest, making them uninviting during Boulder's chilly winters but excellent in the spring and fall.

The rock is a solid, tight-grained Fountain sandstone featured with huecos, nubbins and crimps—smacking more of Eldo than Flagstaff. The superb Tower of Power might just be the best boulder problem of its grade in the Boulder area. Highballs abound, though the landings are often soft and flat. Simply put, the Terrain is a great bouldering area in a beautiful, relaxing setting at the foot of Bear Peak.

Directions: From the intersection of Broadway and Table Mesa in Boulder turn right (west) onto Table Mesa and drive 0.6 miles to Lehigh, where you take a left (south). Drive another 0.8 miles up the big hill and turn right onto Cragmoor Road (the first right past the light at Mesa Elementary School). Drive 0.1 miles west on Cragmoor and park in the dead-end.

From the parking lot walk west and stay right, following the sign for the North Fork Shanahan Trail to its junction with the Mesa Trail. Then head south on the Mesa Trail for five to seven minutes, contouring into, then out of, a drainage. As you climb out and crest a ridge, the trail bends from east to south. Walk roughly 70 yards from this bend to a slight ridge overlooking a grassy bowl. Cruise up this ridge, rock hopping to minimize impact, for one third of a mile to the Bob Boulder. The Animal Chin Boulder and Fairview Boulder are about two minutes northwest of here across a meadow. Expect an approach time of about 45-50 minutes.

MAIN TERRAIN BOULDERS

WANKA ROCK (AKA THE BOB BOULDER)

This is a choice, 17-foot high blob of Fountain Sandstone plopped down in a pleasant, sunny meadow just 200 yards southeast of Fairview Boulder. Though the holds are somewhat sharp, most of these problems are "must-dos."

1. Golden Ticket V2 *
Up dishes and crimps on the bulging left side of the south face. Nearly as "rad" as Hobbit in a Blender.

2. Bob's Crack V1 *
Crank past good huecos into the black-stained water groove.

3. Dude's Face V4 ***
Harder than it looks and still a bit mossy. Work past strange fluted rails just left of the rounded arete.

4. Trust Arete V4 ***
Start on #5 then yard left for the arete at the hueco. More fun than Dude's Face.

5. Bob's Wall aka What About Bob? V4 **
Continuous, highball, and interesting on appealing red rock. Punch up to the hueco then move slightly right to finish on crimps. One of Boulder's best.

6. All About Bob V2 *
Up incuts on the right side of the boulder, starting on a white-stained flake and moving right.

Matt Samet on Bob's Wall

FUNK SOUL BOULDER

This is a decent little warm-up block, with kind jugs along its lip to get the big muscle groups working. It features a perfect landing and one of the world's worst lowball traverses. It lies just downhill and south, 50 feet from the Fairview Boulder.

1. Madam Assey V0 *
The fun warm-up slab(s) on the southeast side of the rock.

2. Schnitzel Bock V2 *
The left to right traverse, using the jugs along the lip of the wall and topping out as for #5. Fun and pumpy.

3. Schweinhund V9
A worthless butt-dragging traverse across the bottom three feet of an already diminutive wall. Does bouldering get any stupider than this?

4. Funk Soul Roof V4 *
Sds on chalked-up finger slots, below and slightly left of a jug/ horn in the middle of the northeast face. V1 starting from the horn.

Wilbur ponders the Funky Soul

5. V2
Sds on a purple rail near the wall's right margin, then move up past slopers, finishing just left of two small trees growing out of the boulder.

FAIRVIEW BOULDER

This house-sized block is the rightmost of the two huge boulders in the main area. The top features commanding views of Fairview High School—great if high schools are your thing. There are good problems in the V1 to V5 range on almost all its faces, ranging from the sit-down crimpfests of the northwest face to the high, juggy problems around the front side.

1. GFP V1 *
Girl Friend Problem. Past ripples and horizontals on the southwest corner of the rock.

2. GFT V1
Girl Friend Traverse. Sds on huecos underneath the finish to #3 and reel left on jugs, standing up onto a large, purple ledge feature. Low and uninspiring.

3. Kleine Schlampe V3 * 🌀
Ouch! Start low in the horizontal crack as for #4 and #5 but reel left onto the sharp, crimpy lip, moving around the corner and topping out left of the large ponderosa.

4. Eara Fuchin Schmuckin V3 *** 🚙 👋
The poor-man's Warm-up Roof. Start low in the crack, move left 10 feet, then head up past sloping crimps to a juggy, highball top-out.

5. Shoots and Ladders V4 * 🌀 👣
From low in the crack, punch right onto a gritty sloper then head straight over the bulge above to an easy but dirty finish.

6. Snuff V1
Snuff Love! Sds on the northeast arete, moving right to a horn at the lip behind the large ponderosa tree.

7. Parasol V4 **
The leftmost problem on the low northwest face. Sds on purple undercling blocks then head out the bulge to a funky lip move.

8. Corner V2
Six feet right of #7 is the obvious crack/corner feature covered in pine needles, rat feces and mud. Don't bother.

9. Kenny G's Meat Whistle V5 *
A long name for a short problem. Start on a good purple undercling beneath the undercut roof right of #8, then head up the face on sharp slopers.

10. Plush V5 **

The best and most obvious line on the wall, starting on a rail below the tallest part of the face and moving past a sharp pocket to a sloper with a crystal embedded in its left side.

11. Shag V2 *

The rightmost problem on the wall. Work past pebbles in the seam from a sds on a good rail at knee height.

12. For Her Pleasure V4 *

Sds at a good four-finger left-hand pocket and a sharp bidoigt for the right on the west face, then move past sharp holds on the ribbed bulge.

ANIMAL CHIN BOULDER

This huecoed sandstone behemoth, 10 feet left (southwest) of the Fairview Boulder hosts the area's showcase problem Tower of Power, a sequential, highball journey up a 30-degree overhanging wall on perfect rock, as well as a handful of good highballs.

1. Ejector Seat V5 **

This tricky rig climbs the rounded dihedral feature behind a copse of small pine trees on the south edge of the enormous east face. Start on the right and move left through the corner to a dastardly lip move.

2. Highball/Solo V4 ***

This 20-foot high vertical face is mandatory fare for the highball enthusiast. Begin on left-leaning ramps around the arete from The Tower of Power and move right onto the red face. Thin and pebbly up high.

3. MBT V4

Matt's Bad Traverse. Start as for Tower of Power but traverse right across the entirety of the north face, finishing right around the corner onto the slab. Forty-five feet of awkward, pointless traversing.

4. Tower of Power (aka Miah in a Blender) V10 ****

The striking line up the right side of the hanging arete, starting from a sds on underclings and voyaging through continuous, overhanging territory. A new advent, Flower Tower, goes at V10 and stays on the arete the whole way.

5. It Satisfies V5 **

Boy—does it ever! Begin just right of #3 with a sds at the small crack/corner. Head right to a rail, crank a hard move straight up, then trend right on strange, rampy rock.

6. Under the Influence V2 ***

An awesome jug haul taking the line of least resistance up the middle of the north face. Continuously interesting.

7. Northwest Arete V?

Has this pile even been done—and does anybody care? Friable, mankus and mungy.

8. Trench Mouth V2 *

On the west face, move right along a crack/flake feature into a black streak, then head up on crispy flakes.

9. V3

Up the bulging wall with a slab at its base just right of #8. Crimpy, flaky and horrible.

UPPER TERRAIN BOULDERS

THE LOVE BOAT

These highballs are as close as you'll ever get to cocktail hour on The Love Boat. This enormous gray-green block floats 200 yards uphill (west) of the Main Terrain Boulders, and 100 yards above Terror Slabs Boulder (a 35-foot high boulder with a prominent unclimbed slab on its broad northeast face and a decent V4 on its south side). The Love Boat is only about half developed, with room for some very bold highballs both on its bulging east face and on the impeccable, swirly rock of the perennially shady Nordwand.

1. Southeast Corner V3

What, are you fucking kidding me? Up the rounded southeast arete past dirty horizontals over a hideous slab landing.

2. Hot Buttered Cock Porn V4 **

Harder than it looks, this scary problem moves left across the bulge then goes up behind the large ponderosa pine abutting the east face.

Problems #3-#6 all top out into the obvious bowl 15 feet up before moving left across the big slab. Descend to the west.

3. Tall Boy V3 **

Begin just right of the tree and move past scoops and ledges into the big bowl.

4. Glass Plate V3 *

For genuine scat connoisseurs only! Start four feet right of #3 and move up past laybacks and underclings into the middle of the bowl.

5. Famous V4 **

Move up the smooth red face to a small undercling, then crimp your way into the right side of the bowl.

6. Northeast Corner V7 **

Start on an undercling and follow sharp, shallow dishes near the arete, moving left into #5 to finish.

7. Having a Moment V3 ***

Perhaps the finest highball at the Terrain Boulders. This problem cruises up a series of scoops in the dark, swirly rock right of the highest, blankest part of the north face. Continuous, slopey, and TALL!

8. Fag Hag V2 **

Start on a horizontal rail four feet right of #7 and surmount the slightly mossy bulges above. Good stone.

HAVING A MOVEMENT PART DEUX BOULDER

Two hundred yards southwest and uphill from The Love Boat, this isolated ridgetop area offers a few choice lines on compact red rock. The boulder comprises a small, red spire poking up from the south side of the faint ridgeline.

1. Having a Movement V5 ***

The leftmost problem, on pocketed rock with a hard red veneer. This problem faces southeast.

2. Paulious Maximus V4 *

Sds on the south face, eight feet down and right of #1. Slightly chossy.

3. Uberhangin V3 *

Just right again is this west-facing line up an overhang past pockets.

NORTH TERRAIN BOULDERS

THE MILLENNIUM FALCON

This is an overhanging disc-shaped plate of good, steep sandstone two minutes north of the main area via a faint track crossing the forested gully (also filled with blocks). Excellent thuggy climbing on user-friendly stone. The overhang points east.

1. Hand Solo V3 *

This problem would get an extra * if it didn't have a back-slapper landing at the crux. Start in finger slots around the southeast side of the rock, crank left off an undercling, then huck to the lip.

2. Spewbacca V4 ***

Stellar roof climbing on bizarre but solid holds. Start just right of the pillar/slab abutting the east face with your hands matched on a good flake. V5 if you come in from the low pockets on #3.

3. Princess Layme V4 **

Crank out of the obvious low pockets to the ramp at the lip, then grovel over.

THE EVIL KNIEVEL BOULDER

A less-steep but equally as highball version of The Millennium Falcon about 100 yards due west (uphill) from the Falcon, offering two good problems on interesting stone.

1. Evil Knievel V3 **

Up the left side of the east face, six feet right of a small crack. Long reaches to super-kibby huecos, pods and horns.

2. Evil Twin V5 **

The tallest line on the rock with a big move to a good edge/rail at the top. A little grainy.

DEATH ARETE GROTTO

Closer to the Go-Go than the actual Terrain Boulders, this shady little venue merits a visit on a hot day. Head north through deadfall for two minutes from the Millennium Falcon

1. East Face Center V3 *

Straight up crimps in the middle of the east-facing block forming the right wall of the grotto.

2. The P-Link V6 *

Begin on #3, move left to a slot in the face, then dyno into #1 to finish. Height-dependent.

3. Alpine Pansy V5 ***

The technical, devious and strenuous prow/arete on the right side of the wall. A unique, Font-like feature with an ugly, back-slapper landing.

FLATIRONS SOUTH

Phillip Benningfield on Deuto's Pride, V3, PB Boulders   photo: Josh Deuto

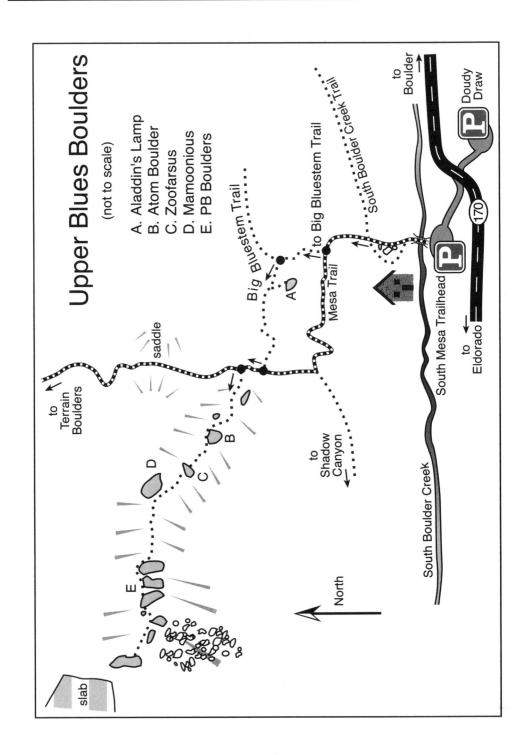

Upper Blues Boulders

(not to scale)

A. Aladdin's Lamp
B. Atom Boulder
C. Zoofarsus
D. Mamoonious
E. PB Boulders

FLATIRONS SOUTH
ALADDIN'S LAMP AND UPPER BLUES BOULDERS

Flatirons bouldering doesn't get much better—or more obscure—than this. These stellar secluded boulders sit in an idyllic grassy gully two canyons south of the Terrain Boulders. Though the approach hike is lengthy, it's not especially steep, and the views of the spires and needles around Shadow Canyon are outstanding. The incredible Mamoonious Boulder offers a plethora of highball problems on impeccable Fountain Sandstone, while a recent find, the PB Boulders, offers stacks of varied problems in a Font-like forest. Expect a good hour's hike!

Directions: Because of erosion, habitat and social trail issues, OSMP is planning on putting a cairned trail from the Terrain Boulders south to the Upper Blues Boulders, thus avoiding the original approach described below. Nevertheless, your first time in to the boulders it might be useful to use the old approach just to get oriented. Please avoid this approach in the fall, when the gully becomes an active bear habitat.

Take Broadway south out of Boulder to the junction with Highway 170 (the Eldorado Market is at this intersection). Turn west to Eldorado Springs. Drive west on Highway 170 for 1.6 miles to the South Mesa Trailhead down and right (an easy turn to miss). Hike north on the Mesa Trail for 20 minutes until you hit the "To Big Bluestem Trail" sign. Follow this cut-off north for about 3-4 minutes to the Big Bluestem Trail (Aladdin's Lamp is about 6-7 minutes up this trail in a small wash just beyond an orderly row of four pine trees to the south), which you then follow west toward the Mesa Trail (another 20-25 minutes).

For the Upper Blues Boulders walk north 60 feet on the Mesa Trail, then cut into the gully diagonaling northwest and up. The boulders are scattered along the length of this gully. The Atom Boulder is about five minutes up the gully, Zoofarsus is about seven minutes, and the enormous Mamoonious sits about 12 minutes up the gully from the trail. The PB Boulders are another three minutes past Mamoonious, heading west on an old trail in the gully.

Alternate approach: From the Bob Boulder at the Terrain Boulders, walk due south along old trail beds for approximately 10 minutes, hugging the base of the steep hillside to the west, to reach Mamoonious. Please reverse this approach when leaving and don't cut east to the Mesa Trail. This approach should be cairned in the near future.

Approach time: one hour.

A. ALADDIN'S LAMP

A curious little cave boulder but well worth a visit on your way to the Upper Blues Boulders. Good landings, juggy rails and a fine southerly exposure make this an excellent bumbling and picnic venue. Hollow but seemingly solid jug-flakes abound.

1. Genie V3 *
From the cave's far left side, traverse right across incuts rails. Finish on #2, 13 feet to the right.

2. Magic Carpet V2 *
Tug on edges up the maroon wall just right of the grass-filled ledge. Sds on the hanging disk.

3. Climb Aladdin V3 *
Crouch-start on the white-stained horizontal then amble up the crimpy face. Many variations possible. V4 if you traverse into it from the left.

UPPER BLUES BOULDERS

B. ATOM BOULDER

This is the first developed boulder in the Upper Blues area and sits in the gully floor 150 feet past a pointy slab/spire on the right. Though the holds are somewhat sharp, the landings are cush and the ripply grips attract the eye.

1. Doodlely Dud V4 *
Sds on pockets in the gray band, then undercling on crystals out the low roof and turn the lip on grungy slopers.

2. Curly Merl V4 *
Start on #1. Traverse the lip of the disk six feet, and finish on crimps right of the little tree.

3. Mighty Dude V4? **
Harder since a hold broke? Start on a low, right-hand sidepull and reef up and left to bad holds over the lip. Burly.

4. Adam's Roof V4 **
Start matched in a positive, white-stained hueco at waist height then move up and left to a sharp slot. V2 if you start in the slot.

5. Teeny Babies V4 *
Bust up the white pebbles, then huff your way up the blunt prow.

6. Jumpin' Gymnee V1
The rounded, mossy northeast arete of the block.

C. ZOOFARSUS

A low, east-facing cave boulder just two minutes up the gully from the Atom Boulder. Though short, the problems offer athletic moves on pocketed purple stone.

1. Zooloo V3
Start on the pockets and crank for a slot, then grunge up and over the nappy lip.

2. Zoofarsus Traverse V6 *
Start far left on a flat jug and traverse across pockets in the roof, finishing far right on the crumbly face. Twenty feet long.

3. Zoo TV V6 **
Gymnastic and fun. Start on #2 and traverse into #4.

4. Zoofarsus Roof V4 *
Sds on the low pocket band and punch straight out the roof to a grainy flake. Thuggy and gymnastic.

D. MAMOONIOUS
This monstrous erratic, blessed with flat piney landings and perfect rock, is way-the-fuck up in the woods, making for a great escape. Horns, flakes, ripples and pockets dot the iron-hard maroon and tan stone on three sides of the boulder. Expect high problems.

SOUTH FACE

1. Chaugle Pants V5 ****
The leftmost line on the south face, starting five feet left of #2 and moving into a scooped dish at the lip of the overhang.

2. South Face Direct V3 ***
Start about eight feet left along the flake and hit a sloper at the lip, then move up the varnished face above to a good pocket. Finish out the upper bulge for full value.

3. Crystal Reach V3 **
From the bottom of the flake fire up and right to the obvious jug crystal then cruise up the face above.

4. Mamoonious Flake V3 *
Climb along the flake/crack on the steep southwest side of the boulder, moving left around the corner to finish. Pumpy.

5. Easy Skeazin V0 **
The downclimb. The path of least resistance on the buckets right of the crystal.

6. Crimp-Wah V4 **
Sds six feet left of the southeast arete on slopers, then pimp your way up tinies to the good, maroon jug rail.

7. Southeast Arete V7 **** 😊

Climb the prominent nose, off-routing the jug rails out left and using the textured sloper instead. Top out direct via the committing bulge.

8. Traverse V6 ** 😊

Start on #6 and move left (west) across the wall, staying low on crimpers then moving high on the diagonaling slopers to finish on #2 (without stepping down to the flake). Pumpy and technical.

SOUTHEAST FACE

9. Southeast Wall V5 *** 😊

The excellent maroon face. Start standing on the block and fire up and right to an incut, then trend back left along the diagonal seams. Can also be started further left.

10. East Arete V4 ** 😊

Start on #9 but go straight up to funky pockets over the lip, finishing up in the rounded groove. Freakous.

EAST FACE

11. Mamoonia V3 *

Climb flakes in the bulging, black streak just left of the long white stain. Worthy.

12. Moonbeam V6 *

The diagonaling seam six feet right of #10. Hard to achieve lift-off.

13. Squeezin' and Skeezin' V4 *

A difficult line just left of the large tree growing against the northeast face. Start with your right hand on a good flake/sidepull.

E. THE PB BOULDERS

Discovered in spring 2001, this recent find makes the approach trudge to the Blues Boulders all the more worthwhile, adding a tightly grouped cluster of six impressive boulders to this gully. Surrounded by trees, these sandstone blocks are mostly shady, providing a good venue on warmer days. Problems vary from highballs to fun slabs and pumpy overhangs, almost all on perfect rock. Walk three steep minutes up the gully from Mamoonious.

BOULDER #1

The enormous, glassy boulder at the bottom (east side) of the cluster. It's the first boulder you'll encounter.

1. Undone V? **

Climb the clean southeast arete on the super-aesthetic south face of the boulder. Big reaches to little crimps on a flat, overhanging wall.

BIG ORANGE (BOULDER #2)

This is the giant block just uphill and west with its characteristic, highball, orange-colored north face. Two must-do problems on Eldo-hard stone await the intrepid!

2. Big Orange V1 ** 🚗

The tall face. Start on the right in a faint groove and work left on the jugs, topping out on the left side of the face past a white-stained flake.

3. Kurious Oranj V6 * 🚗 ⏱**

Sds on the block, your left hand on the good horizontal edge, then work straight up the face on crimps to a lunge move. Top out direct to finish.

4. Orange Groove V0 *

The easy groove on the right side of the north face.

THE SAG WAGON (BOULDER #3)

Another super-sized block just west again, easily recognized by its flat, highball, black-colored west face. The dueling highballs on the monolithic west face will loosen your stool and the corner on the north side offers a good challenge for the aspiring hardperson.

5. Sag and Bag V5 *

Low-baggins. Sds on opposing pinch holds on the south side of the boulder left of the tree. Out the cave and up the slab.

6. Deuto's Pride V3 ** 🚗

The rightmost problem on the west face, working past an undercling flake to jugs.

7. Black Wall V5 * 🚗 ⏱**

The central line on the face, starting from a sds and working right from the left-trending ramp up the black wall.

8. Corner V8 ** ⏱

The overhanging dihedral on the north side from a sds. Would get another star if the boulder out right weren't so annoyingly close.

THE SLAB WAGON (BOULDER #4)

The next boulder west with the high, slabby, licheny faces. With some travel these problems should end up being fairly fun.

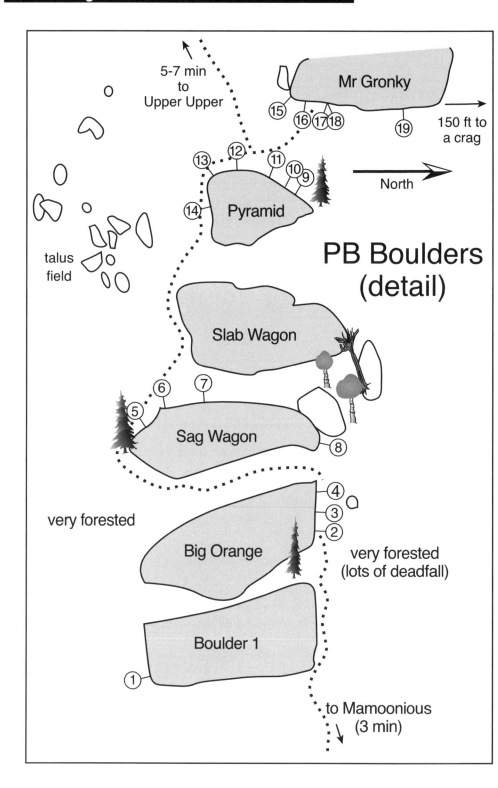

5-7 min
to
Upper Upper

Mr Gronky

15 16 17 18 19

150 ft to
a crag

13 12 11 10 9

North

14 Pyramid

talus
field

PB Boulders
(detail)

Slab Wagon

6 7

5

Sag Wagon

8

very forested

4
3
2

Big Orange

very forested
(lots of deadfall)

Boulder 1

1

to Mamoonious
(3 min)

THE PYRAMID (BOULDER #5)

This pleasing, pyramidal block stands alone, just above the lower four blocks, and features good slab and arete problems on which to warm up.

9. The Downclimb V0-
This is the groove feature just right of the arete on the boulder's west face.

10. Arete Master V1
The blunt arete feature just right of #9.

11. Phillip's Slab V2 *
The left-of-center line up the west face on small sharpies.

12. Undone Slab V2 **
A harder but similar line up the right side of the wall.

13. Arete Meister V0+ *
The sharp southwest arete, featuring a slightly mossy top-out. Fun.

14. South Face V3 ** 😦
An engaging line on the aesthetic, lichen-streaked south face. Start low on sidepulls and yank for a jug over the small roof, then move up the wall above.

MR. GRONKY (BOULDER #6)

This is the highest boulder in the cluster and just uphill and right (north) 40 feet from The Pyramid. It's also the best boulder in the cluster, with tall—but not highball—problems on splitter purple and maroon stone.

15. Funkarete V4 **
The left arete of the boulder from a sds. Gymnastic.

16. Slickhedral V5 **
Sds with a small but incut right-hand flake then head up the obtuse, slippery dihedral. Puzzling.

Phillip spotted by Matt on One Trick Pony   photo: Josh Deuto

17. One Trick Pony V5 ***
Sds on the lower left end of the purple plate and move left to the arete feature, which you follow back right until you can roll over the lip.

18. The Full Gronky V7 ****
An unrelenting pumpfest on smooth, purple slopers. Start on #17 but traverse right along the horizontal limb of the purple plate, finishing on #19.

19. Mr. Gronky V5 ***
The vertical limb of the purple plate. Sds and bear-hug your way up this crazy feature to a taxing lip encounter.

Matt Samet on the Full Gronky

ELDORADO CANYON

Eldorado Springs Canyon

Boulder's most famous and historic climbing venue has long been host to a myriad of good boulder problems, yet only recently have climbers begun developing the large, promising blocks up and out of the canyon proper. With its enchanting ambience, solid rock, and unexplored bouldering possibilities, good old Eldo promises to keep yielding great new problems in the years to come. The rock, subject to different geologic forces than the rest of the Fountain formation in the nearby Flatirons, is generally bullet hard—sometimes so bullet it's blank!

Directions: Drive south on Highway 93 (Broadway) out of Boulder, to the junction with Highway 170, (1.7 miles south of the last stoplight in town, at Greenbriar). Turn right and drive 3.1 miles west through the town of Eldorado Springs to the park entrance, where you must pay a $5 daily entrance fee ($50 for an annual Colorado State Parks pass, valid also at Castlewood Canyon).

Parking Beta:

For the East Draw: Park in the lowest lots just inside the Park and walk back east across the bridge to the Springs. There is no public parking in the town.

For the Whale's Tail and the Wisdom Simulator Simulator: Park in one of the lower lots just past the entrance station.

For West World: Drive roughly 0.4 miles up the canyon and park at the road-side Milton Boulder on the right, when the creek is low or frozen, otherwise park in one of the lower lots and approach via the West Ridge Trail.

For the Eldorado Canyon Trail Boulders (Pony Keg, Musical Boulders and Nightmare Block): Drive 0.7 miles up the canyon and park at the Gill Boulder on the right (just over the bridge) or continue west toward the Ranger Station (the low road) and park in one of the lots there.

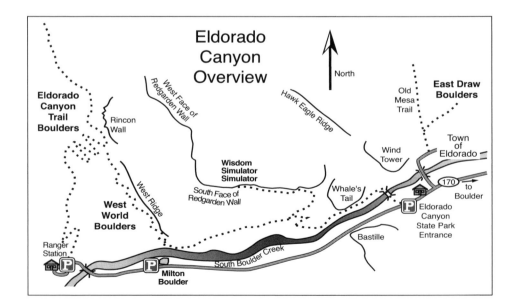

Eldorado Canyon Overview

112

EAST DRAW

Perched on the sunny hogback above the quiet town of Eldorado Springs, these secluded boulders saw only sporadic action until they were "rediscovered" by Eldo residents Eric Johnson and Chip Ruckgaber in the fall of 2000. Home to the Couch Potato, a 5.12 toprope wall dating back to the 80's, this sheltered ridge is a perfect winter destination, catching sun until early evening and melting out quickly after snowstorms. The rock varies from bullet Dakota to a pebbly sort of hand-eating conglomerate reminiscent of the more rubbly stuff at Pile Tor or Biglandia 40 miles north. Though the boulders are on public land, access is somewhat tricky and your every move can be seen and heard from the town below. Best to limit your group size and maintain a low profile!

Directions: Drive west through the town of Eldorado Springs and park in the lower lot in the Park. Walk back east across the bridge, hang a left across the other bridge to the Springs then follow the road east as it goes behind the pool. Just after the pool the road splits into three; take the middle fork, heading uphill and east through a trailer park. Follow the road back around behind the trailer park (west) until it forks again into two driveways. Walk 100 feet up the righthand driveway, then take the trail that heads off right onto the hillside (this is the Old Mesa Trail). Follow the trail 50 yards to a large pine tree, then branch right on a faint climber's trail and make your way up the hill as best you can.

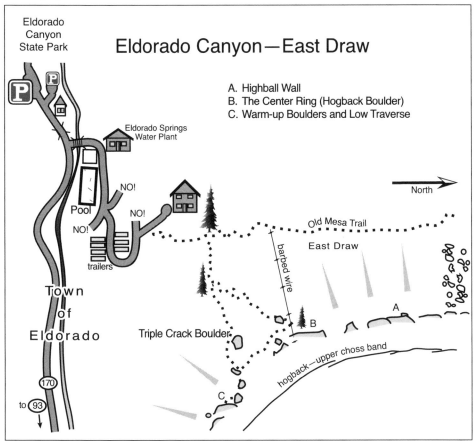

Eldorado Canyon State Park

Eldorado Canyon—East Draw

A. Highball Wall
B. The Center Ring (Hogback Boulder)
C. Warm-up Boulders and Low Traverse

Eldorado Springs Water Plant

North

NO!
Pool
NO!
NO!
trailers

Old Mesa Trail
East Draw
barbed wire

T o w n
o f
E l d o r a d o

Triple Crack Boulder

A
B
C

hogback—upper choss band

170
to 93

A. HIGHBALL WALL

Tall problems with committing moves and butt-clenching top-outs, well above a grassy landing. This diamond-shaped wall is approximately 60 yards northwest of the Center Ring, just past an equally appealing toprope up a tall black face. The left sector of the wall over the terrible block landing has yet to see a ropeless ascent.

1. Pervertical Sanctuary V2 * 🚙

Climb the left side of the diamond-shaped wall via an incipient crack, moving right onto #3 to finish.

2. D1 V4 ** 🚙

The direct line up the middle of the diamond. From the horizontal rail, two feet above the small roof, move left onto crimps and laybacks in the burnished patch of tan rock.

3. King of Swords V2 *** 🚙

The right side of the wall. Continuous climbing on good holds past a sinker pocket to a bizarre, disconcerting top-out. Twenty-plus feet tall.

B. THE CENTER RING (AKA THE HOGBACK BOULDER)

This varied wall of rugged conglomerate is the main hang in the East Draw, offering a 60-foot, schralper traverse and a handful of good up-problems. To get there wend your way northeast up the hill, eventually crossing an old barbed-wire fence up high. The fence abuts the right end of the wall.

1. Hooey's Back Porch V3 * 🚙

A bad name for a fun problem. Start on the sloping horizontal at arm's length on the wall's left end and reel straight up over the lip to a hidden finger pocket. V8 ** from a low-as-you-can-go sit start.

2. V3 *

Same start as #1 but reel right along the lip, topping out past a loose-looking block feature.

Eric Johnson sends King of Swords

3. Pig-Dog V6 ***

One of the steeper problems on the Front Range, taking a tempting line of holds out a flat, 30-degree overhanging wall. Sit start, ass in the dirt, left hand in a four-finger pocket, right hand on a sidepull, then go straight out the overhang.

4. Crack V2
Start on #3 but crank right along the painful, pebbly crack under the roof.

5. Pig's Nose V3 **
A superb jug haul! Start just right of #3, sitting down with your right hand in a deep, incut letterbox. Crank past horizontals and the pig's nose to good holds at the lip.

Matt Samet on Hooey's Back Porch photo: Josh Deuto

6. Slopers V3 *
Climb the face on the right side of the wall, 10 feet left of the big tree, via glassy slopers. Challenging.

7. Undercling Mantle V2
The face just right of #6, starting on funky holds in the brown rock and hitting mossy jugs at the lip.

8. Barb-Wire Traverse V7 *
Sixty feet long and very rugged. Begin as far right as possible, just left of the ponderosa. Stay low (five feet and under) through the beginning and middle on funky horns, slopers and pockets to finish out on #5. Knee-bar rests are on. The traverse into #3 is Pig Dog Girl V9/10 **.

C. WARM-UP BLOCKS
This trio of Carter-lake-style cubes of brown and green sandstone is situated along the hillside down (60-70 yards) and southeast of the Center Ring. As the name implies, this is a great place to warm up.

BLOCK ONE
This block has a challenging, crimpy problem on its southeast face and a handful of mossy slabs (V0-V2) on its northwest side.

Block One

1. Crimpy Face V5 **

A steeper-than-it-looks type problem on the aesthetic southeast face. Start just right of the arete on pebbly crimpers, make a big move up and right to another set of crimps, then finish out past the loose flake (no grab!) in the black rock.

2. V3 *

The stand-up finish to #1, moving to the jug at mid-height from a crisp, right-hand under-cling.

BLOCK TWO

This block faces almost due south, making it a good place to catch morning sun on your warm-up circuit. Melts out quickly.

1. Left Side V2 *

Climb the tan rock right of the arete, eventually moving left around the arete into a finger crack.

2. Black Dike V1 *

The most pleasant line on the wall, Follow the pebbly, black striation just left of the center.

3. Scoop-Face V3 *

Climb the scoop feature in the center of the wall, starting with your left hand on an under-cling and your right hand on a good sidepull, then up the grainy face above.

4. Right Arete V2 *

Start with a chest-high right-hand crimp around the corner then slap up to the big plate on the left and mantle over.

5. Overhanging Crack V1

The steep crack/flake feature around the corner from the arete.

BLOCK THREE

This 20-foot high block leans against the top of the Low Traverse, forming a small alcove.

1. Crack V0+

Climb the loose, spooky, right-leaning crack up the left side of the southwest face.

2. Face V2 **

Trend diagonally right across the big face, passing a couple of ledges en route to the mortifyingly technical top-out.

3. Scoop V2 * 😊 🤚

This career-ending line takes the scoop and arete on the right side of the block over the terrible landing. Committing, though not especially difficult.

D. LOW TRAVERSE

This excellent power-endurance problem on the steep, recessed wall abutting the lowest of the Warm-up Blocks is a good place to finish off, as the holds are much smoother than those at the other walls.

1. Crack V2 **

The excellent finger-to-hand crack on the left side of the wall. Start sitting down on the horn for full value.

2. Face V4 *

The dark-brown face just right of the crack. Shoulder roll from the horn to a left-hand mini-horn, then punch straight out the bulge on good holds.

3. Traverse V6 ***

Begin far right on a good block then cruise left past flat holds to reach a sloping ledge, which you follow to #1. Top out via the crack. Finishing left past the crack on glassy slopers adds 12 feet of climbing and a V-grade. Aesthetically pleasing. Pleasingly aesthetic.

E. TRAILSIDE BOULDER

This squatty, isolated boulder is actually in the bottom of the East Draw, another four minutes north up the Old Mesa Trail. Though not as sunny as its counterparts on the ridge, this rock offers a hard, hueco-esque line up the south overhang just off the trail.

1. Trailside Overhang V7 **

Start low on the creaky flake and work your way past slopers and crimps to the lip. Thuggy and unique. A thuggy anomaly.

ELDORADO CANYON

WHALE'S TAIL UPDATE
CREEK BOULDER

This hidden gem of a boulder sits just below the retaining wall along the walkway at the base of the Whale's Tail, about 20 feet downstream (east) of the Monument cave.

1. Three Feet High and Rising V7 ** 🖐

This fine problem climbs the left side of the east face using a series of crimpy layback holds for the right hand and eventually hitting the slopey lip over the slab landing. As the name implies, this problem is inaccessible during high water.

MILTON BOULDER AND WEST WORLD UPDATE

Home to the mega-classic Germ Free Adolescence, this steep, slippery hillside of polished blocks has seen a few good new problems go in over the course of the 2000-2001 season. Although there aren't many good moderate problems to warm-up on and landings tend toward the sloping, this area is still worth a visit, mostly for the tall pine and quiet maroon block ambience. Though south-facing, this hillside is also quite wooded; landings can be sloppy and wet a day or two after big snowstorms, but the rock is quick to dry.

Directions: Drive west through the town of Eldorado Springs into the Park and park at the Milton Boulder (during low water, or when the creek is frozen over). For West World, cross the creek via a series of slippery rocks just downstream from Milton and head straight up the hill and left (west) to the boulders. Alternately, when the creek is high, park at the lower lot in the Park and approach as for the West Ridge, heading left across the hill to the boulders once you've made the greasy traverse on the slabs just above the creek. Approach time: five to ten minutes.

PETE'S PROW BOULDER

This is the north-facing, prow shaped boulder directly across the road from the Milton Boulder.

1. Pete's Prow V5 * 🖐

Slap moves to glassy slopers take you up this tricky rig on the double aretes. A harder, low start awaits an ascent …

WEST WORLD

PARK TECH BOULDER

This is a tiny block with fun problems and good landings, nestled in a flat pine grove just 50 feet from the creek, about 150 feet upstream (west) of the Milton Boulder on the opposite side of the creek.

1. Left Side V4 ⬤

Sds on the horizontal and move right then back left into the funky seam over the "interactive anal block."

2. Tone's Warm-up V2 *

From the same sds go right and up the crack.

3. Park Tech V5 **

From the crimps on the right side of the wall make a big toss to the sinker hueco at the lip. A V6 variation moves right a few feet from the start on sharp crimpers.

ROOFUS BOULDER

This is the large boulder with a high, south-facing slab 50 feet left (west) of the Germ Free Boulder. Clean angles and smooth rock give this block character.

1. When the Chips are Down V9 *** ⬤

This stellar new line, put up by Colin Lantz in the fall of 2000, takes the high, lichen-streaked face right of Sheep Thrills on the boulder's west face. Start on the rockpile/wall and move into a finger lock, then make a long throw up and right for a sloping rail.

2. Colin's Highball V2 * ⬤⬤

This ultra-sandbag rating was provided by the first ascensionist. Start on the old V0+ in the scoop on the right side of the west face then work back left along the lip of the ramping arete.

3. High Slab V0 * ⬤⬤

Step onto the southwest arete of the boulder from the big block, then realm up the mono-lithic southern slab above. Harder if you stay left on the small edges.

GERM FREE BOULDER

This is the obvious roof/cave boulder in the middle of the hillside.

1. Twisted Adolescence V8 * ⬤

This powerful variation climbs out the cave just left of Germ Free Adolescence. Start on Germ Free but take the flake/hueco with your right hand and bust high and left to a three-finger pocket, then the lip.

TRUTH BLOCK

This recently unearthed little gem reveals its charms only upon close inspection … meaning don't just write it off as another anonymous frumpy pile. The crimpy, positive nature of the rock and the boulder's sunny position above the creek make for a good outing. This boulder is roughly 100 feet below the Germ Free Boulder and about 60 feet above the creek.

1. Truth or Dare V4 * ◔

A crimpy problem in the slot on the left (west) side of the boulder, starting from two good square-cut edges at head height.

2. Dare V2 * ◔

Start on the incut flake and move left over the drop-off. Mega scary!

3. Nice Move V3 ◔

Start on the same incut flake and punch up and right to a sloper.

4. Truth V4 ** ◔

The center line up the southeast face, topping out just right of the big dead tree. Sds for extra value. A V5 ** traverse starts on Truth and crimps rightward 13 feet to finish on a rounded purple horn.

5. Lies V1 ◔

Start from the rampy rock and climb the short wall via sidepulls.

WEST RIDGE TRAVERSE

Though somewhat friable, this fun traverse provides a good lactic burn on interesting blocky stone. It's also a decent place to mess around and warm-up, as the holds tend to be bigger than the unforgiving crimps of West World. The traverse is at the lower (southern) end of the West Ridge about 100 feet above the creek.

1. West Ridge Traverse V5 **

Traverse the diagonaling break from right to left, either finishing direct up the steep face via chossy holds on the traverse's left end or simply stepping off. The Terminator Version, V6 *, starts all the way down and right and crosses the lower wall on sharp crystals to join the traverse.

THE WISDOM SIMULATOR SIMULATOR

This esoteric, somewhat intimidating slot problem follows a continuous line of small but positive holds along the lip of the slot cave between Dangerous Acquaintances and The Wisdom on the upper (west) end of the Roof Wall. A good place to climb if you're already up there ...

1. Wisdom Simulator Simulator V8 **

Approach as for the Roof Wall routes. This problem is in the upper slot just above the approach slab used to reach Rosy Crucifixion. Start on a good, flat jug up and left of Dangerous Acquaintances and traverse 60 feet up and left along the lip of the slot, stepping off where the wall turns slabby at the base of the first pitch of The Wisdom. Needs traffic.

Charley Bentley dicing up the High Slab (V0-) on Roofus Rock   photo: Matt Samet

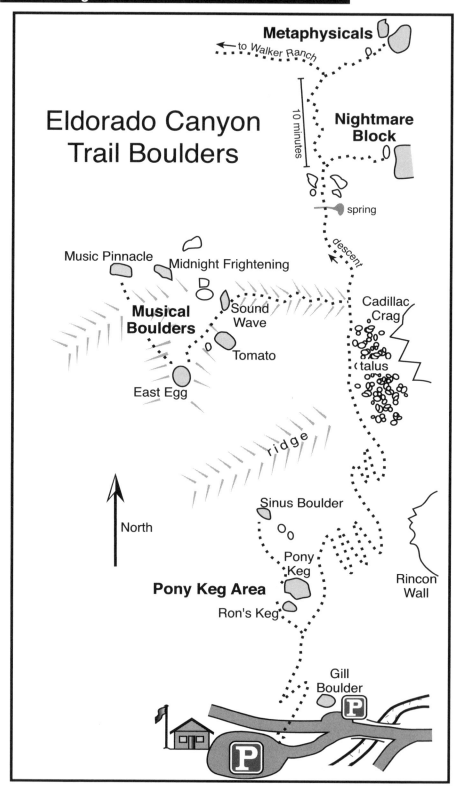

Metaphysicals

← to Walker Ranch

Eldorado Canyon
Trail Boulders

10 minutes

Nightmare
Block

spring

descent

Music Pinnacle

Midnight Frightening

Musical
Boulders

Sound
Wave

Cadillac
Crag

talus

Tomato

East Egg

ridge

North

Sinus Boulder

Pony
Keg

Rincon
Wall

Pony Keg Area

Ron's Keg

Gill
Boulder

P

P

ELDORADO CANYON TRAIL BOULDERS
THE RON AND PONY KEGS, AND THE MUSICAL BOULDERS

Though technically two separate areas, these two clusters of rock are similar enough and close enough together to combine into a single circuit. Blessed with perfect landings in grassy meadows, clean maroon stone, and a kind southerly exposure, both areas are quick to melt out after snowstorms and offer pleasant, quiet getaways from urban encroachment. Given their very sunny exposure and the crimpy nature of the problems, these boulders are best visited from October through April.

Directions: For both the Pony Keg and the Musical Boulders take the Eldorado Canyon Trail, which heads up and north out of the western end of the park. For Ron's Keg and the Pony Keg follow the trail up past two switchbacks then north along a split-rail fence. The fence soon ends. Just before a set of new wooden steps, head left into the grassy, open gully below the burn area on the ridge to the west.
Approach time: five minutes.

RON'S KEG

Though short and somewhat sharp, this sunny blob of maroon rock plopped down in a soft meadow is not without merit. Combine the short approach with perfect landings and a crack at the harder problems on the adjacent Pony Keg to sweeten the deal.

1. Chip's Arete V2 *
Climb the slabby, rounded northwest arete via thin sharpies.

2. Ron's Keg Traverse V5 **
Start on #1 and traverse right across the entire rock, cruising past the hueco on the south face to finish out on #8. Tricky.

3. Easy Crack V0
Amble up the fun crack four feet right.

4. Horn's Mudda V2 *
Start on the good horn and move up and left to a pinch. Moving right and up to the small pine tree is V1 and slightly crumbly.

5. Southwest Arete V2 *
Climb the arete/prow starting around its south side and working your way past crimps to a good horn.

6. South Face V3

Start with your right hand on the undercling seam and fire up and left to a sloping pocket, then top out via sharp crimpers. Painful and unnecessary.

7. Direct South Face V5 **

Start in the lone hueco and move up and right to a small slit pocket, then surmount the glassy bulge as best you can. Unruly.

8. V0-

Climb the short but appealing water groove on the right side of the south face via pockets and layaways.

Eric Johnson on The Walrus, East Egg   photo: Josh Deuto

Pony Keg

This glassy chunk of maroon stone took on an even redder hue in the summer of 2000, when slurry bombers inundated the area in effort to contain a nearby wildfire. After that the already slippery holds took on an even glossier sheen. Nevertheless, the improbable lines on this rock provide a unique challenge.

1. Left Side V2
Start on the head-high jug rail where the angle changes on the north face and traverse five feet left on crimps, then head up the slab. Weird.

3. Center Route V4 **
This is the easiest way up the foothold-free north face. Start with your left hand on a good incut at head-height and your right hand in the horizontal three feet to the right, then slap over the bulge for a dish.

4. Fingertip Traverse V6 **
Start on the northwest corner and move left along the obvious seam, topping out 20 feet left when the wall turn slabby on #1. Thuggy and annoyingly devoid of footholds.

5. The High Traverse V5 *
Traverse the slopey lip of the wall.

6. Northwest Corner V5 *
Start on the large crystal right of the crack/seam and crank rightwards over the bulge on sharp edges, off-routing the crack to the left. The crack itself is V1.

7. Woody's Pebble V3
The sharpest boulder problem on earth! Surmount the bulge just left of the southwest arete, off-routing the good holds in the crack and tugging on a shark-tooth crystal. Horrible, awful, execrable.

8. The Rail V2 **
Sds on the southwest arete at the crack, then reel right along the crack for 20 feet until the rock turns slabby. Easier up-problems can also be done along the length of the south face.

9. Pony Keg Traverse V8+ **
Reverse #7 and cross the west face of the boulder using the horizontal seam and a set of crimps just above it to finish out on #4. Continuous and technical—meaning your feet are gonna slop off. Sicker V-grade glory awaits those who off-route the holds above the seam.

THE MUSICAL BOULDERS

Though not particularly extensive, these isolated boulders, when combined with a trip to either the Nightmare Block or the Pony Keg, are part of one of Boulder's better adventure-bouldering circuits. Their sunny aspect high on a ridge below Cadillac Crag guarantees quick meltage after winter snowstorms, with potential for new problems as well.

Directions: For the Musical Boulders continue on the Eldorado Canyon Trail another 20 minutes until you hit the open ridge which leads down to the boulders.
Approach time: 30 minutes.

EAST EGG

This lone erratic perched high on a scenic ridge (and visible from the ridge above the Pony Keg) is a mandatory stop for highball and thin-face aficionados. The Walrus, a perfect line on exemplary Eldorado stone, is a must-do for the grade, and the tall slabs around the southwest side of the boulder provide stimulating highball entertainment.

1. Downclimb V0-
The easiest way up and down the rock. Climb the high, slabby northwest face.

2. Slab I V1 *
Start four feet left of the vibrant, green lichen on good huecos, climbing the rounded bulge to a slightly reachy top-out.

3. Slab II V2 **
The center line on the wall, heading up the tallest shield of rock to finish out directly below a small pine tree. You can bail either right or left if you get gripped up high.

4. Slab III V1 *
Locate the huecos in the black streak seven feet left of the arete. Head straight up on slightly friable flakes and nubbins.

5. Southern Prow V0 **
Climb the high, rampy prow where the east face meets the southwest slabs. A mini-solo.

6. The Walrus V5 **** 🫠
One of Boulder's finest, to be sure. Climb the faint black streak up the blankest part of the east face, starting with your right hand on an undercling flake. Continuously thin and committing up high.

7. Eggman V3 ** 🫠
This classic line climbs the vibrant, green lichen streak up the middle of the east face, starting from a small, round boulder at the base. Finish up the faint water groove on the left for Tone's Variation, V3.

8. Steak Knife V4 *
Climb the slightly mossy face five feet left of the northeast arete. Quite thin.

THE WORLD'S SMALLEST BOULDER
This diminutive blob is 100 feet uphill and northeast of the East Egg. No spotter required.

1. Shortest Hardest V3 *
The line up the bulging left side of the west face to a mantle crux at the lip.

2. Shortest Easiest V1
Sds on pockets and climb the southwest face via nice red stone.

3. Shortest Medium V2 *
Actually sort of fun for a lowly lowball. Sds on the bottom, southern end of the diagonaling seam on the east face and follow it rightwards to a roofy conclusion.

THE TOMATO
This rounded red orb just uphill of The World's Smallest Boulder offers similar problems on frustratingly bald stone.

THE MUSIC PINNACLE
Head due north from the East Egg 100 yards into the trees to find this appealing boulder, the lowest of the northernmost cluster of boulders. Expect high problems with thin, sharp holds.

1. West Crack V5 ** 🫠
Sds low and left on small pockets then work up and right into the twin crack/groove systems, eventually jamming the rightmost one to finish.

2. Pinnacle Crack V0 * 🚗

This is the obvious crack/corner line on the south face. It's also the best way off the boulder.

3. Sherman's Seam V1 ** 🚗

The leftmost line on the east face and also the most obvious. Follow the seam/faint dihedral up slick rock to the top of the boulder.

4. Funk V3 * 🚗

Just right of the seam climb the faint arete feature with pockets, entering it from the scoop on the right. Thin and technical.

5. East Face Center V3 * 🚗 ✋

Follow the scoop all the way to the top, tugging on thin crimps and suspect crystals en route. Beware the ankle-breaker landing on embedded rocks.

6. East Face Arete V2 * 🚗 ✋

Move right out of the scoop onto the round arete then slap right for a good edge up high. Leads you on ...

LIGHTNING SPIRE (AKA HERTZ ROCK)

This block sits 30 feet east and uphill from the Music Pinnacle. When completed, the striking line on its east face will be one of Boulder's best and hardest.

1. Midnight Frightening V? **** 🚗

This line has yet to be climbed directly up the scoop but may have been done starting on the crack to the left. The arete to the right is also unclimbed.

SOUND WAVE BOULDER

Though low and squatty, this block is blessed with perfect Eldo sandstone and fun huecos, pinch ribs, and crimps along its overhanging east face. Walk east and uphill from the Lightning Spire about 50 yards, passing a huge perched boulder en route.

1. Sound Wave Traverse V4 **

Traverse the east face from right to left, either finishing out on its south end where it turns slabby or staying low around the corner and topping out via a cobbled alcove on the west side.

C. NIGHTMARE BLOCK

This hunk of 20-foot-high and 15-degree-overhanging maroon sandstone offers steep, powerful climbing in a secreted-away, forested setting. Most of the block's monolithic west face is composed of dark maroon rock laced with sidepulls, incuts and spikes, similar to the rock on Eldo's classic sport route Your Mother (12d). The ten-odd up-problems, numerous variations and two traverses will have you pumped hellishly fast—the rock is very smooth, and you'll find yourself over-gripping, especially on the higher problems. The arduous approach (30-40 minutes uphill) is a great idiot-barrier, making this a wonderful place to come when you want to be left the fuck alone.

Approach: Walk 100 yards on the upper road leading west from the Gill Boulder until you hit the Eldorado Canyon Trail. After two quick switchbacks the trail levels out and heads north. After passing a split rail fence on the left, you'll see a faint trail leading down and left to the Pony Keg boulder. Stay on the main trail past another nine switchbacks (passing the cut-off to Rincon Wall at the fifth switchback). A couple of minutes up from the last switchback you'll cross the grassy ridge leading down to the Musical Boulders and East Egg.

The trail levels out then drops down through a talus field shaded by large ponderosa pines. Pass a marker in the trail, then a small spring five yards further along with a culvert running under the trail. Hike another 35 yards, passing through a cluster of boulders, then turn right (east) and hike uphill 50 yards along a faint ridge, coming to the Nightmare Block, a west-facing, 10- to 20-foot-high maroon wall.

Approach time: 30-40 thigh-burning minutes.

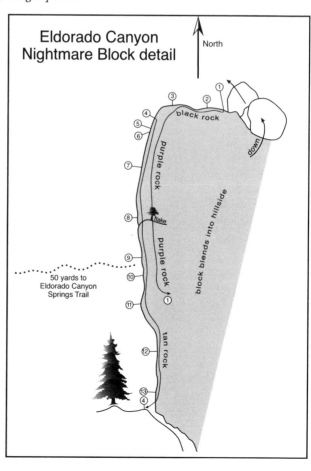

Eldorado Canyon
Nightmare Block detail

North

black rock

purple rock

block blends into hillside

flake

purple rock

50 yards to
Eldorado Canyon
Springs Trail

tan rock

down

NORTH FACE

1. Cameron's Way V5 *

A lip traverse of the entire block. Begin atop the easternmost boulder stacked against the north face of the block (you use this boulder to descend from the problems) and step onto the wall, sagging low onto a slopey rail that leads you down to the top of #2. Hand traverse around the corner, staying on the lip of the wall until you reach #8, then mantle.

2. One Move Makes You Wonder V4 **

Start in the whitish corner above a rocky landing and fire up and right to a jug at the lip. V7 from a low start, down and right.

3. All Dogs Must Die V3 **

Just big wet stupid ones. Begin above the perfect landing just left of the arete on underclings and fire for an edge. V6 from a low start.

WEST FACE

4. Nightmare Traverse V10 ****

One of the best power-endurance problems in the Front Range. This 45-foot traverse isn't so bad move-for-move, but the pump factor is hideous. Stay roughly below eight-foot height, beginning on the left arete (#5) and finishing out by stepping off the slab on the wall's south end. Unrelenting, shouldery, and tough.

5. Derek and the Sentinel V2 *

The line up the arete, moving right on slopers to an awkward top-out.

Eric Johnson conversing with his liver   photo: Matt Samet

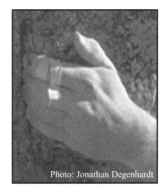

6. Gumby Hell V2 *
Start on the arete but punch right to large sidepulls, topping out as for #5. Fun in a weird-ass, barn-door sort of way.

7. One Cigarette Makes it Murder V5 **
Six feet right of Gumby Hell, this fine, powerful problem makes its way past sloping gastons, sidepulls and an obvious pinch rib into a set of twin cracks that meet in a V-notch at the lip. V7 from a sds on a large, left-facing undercling.

8. Standard Nightmare V5 **** 😎
The directissima of the wall and perhaps its purest line. Start just right of the obvious pinch rail on #6 and punch up past slopers into jugs. Pant-loader exit.

9. Salvator V3 *** 😎
Almost as good as the Standard Nightmare, the direct line cruises up incuts and sidepulls in the faint, diagonaling seams on the right side of the maroon plaque. V4 from the sds.

10. My Liver Talks to Me V6 ** 😎
Sds directly under the faint arete where the purple plaque of rock meets the brown sandstone on the right. Grunt your way past crimpers and sidepulls without using the right arete, heading for the jug 15 feet up on #9.

11. The Optimator V3 *** 😎
Begin just right of #9 at the border between the maroon and the tan rock, then crank past sidepulls, spikes, and a crimper on the right to a juggy but tricky top-out. V4 with a sds.

12. You Can Do It V1 * 😎
Well, maybe. Start on the juggy spikes seven feet left of the right margin of the block. Climb past a faint corner, then move left on the slab to top out. The area "warm-up."

13. Ants V2 * 😎
Start as for #11 but head straight up the slab right of the corner. Crimpy in the slabbiest of ways.

THE METAPHYSICAL BOULDERS
Extra-super bonus blocks for those who just can't get enough steep hiking! Continue another 10 minutes along the Eldorado Canyon Trail from the Nightmare Block to the point at which the trail makes its final bend westward toward Walker Ranch. The trail passes over a small wooden bridge in the bottom of a steep ravine leading northeast. Either follow the ravine or better, hike along the right lip of the ravine for roughly 6-9 minutes until you encounter a cluster of house-sized blocks. An obvious classic, Seven Inch Gumby V5 ***, climbs the right side of the tall, purple wall on the lower block. The middle block offers fun slab and traverse problems in the V1-V6 range, and the upper block offers an ultra-highball V4 called Pocahontas up the pocketed wall just left of the obvious, blank overhang. There are more boulders up the hill; the potential for futuristic highballs at this area is just beginning to be tapped.

Please be aware that this area is under study by the City of Boulder Open Space and Mountain Parks and that access issues could arise.

CLEAR CREEK CANYON

"Fat" Samet is Up With People   photo: Josh Deuto

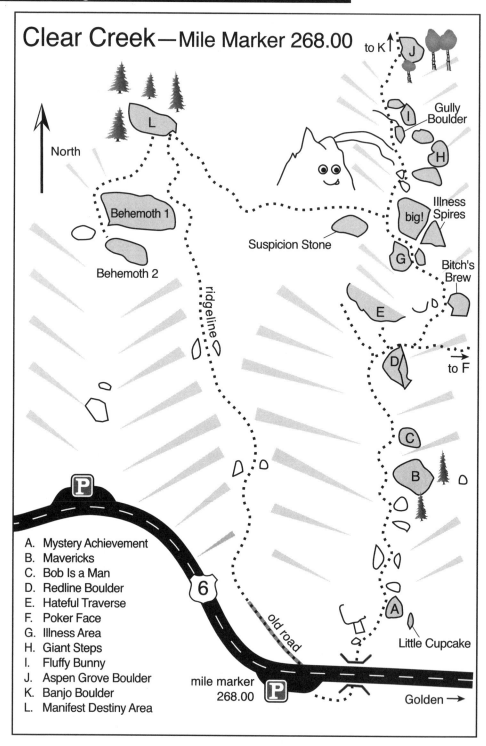

Clear Creek—Mile Marker 268.00

to K

J

North

L

Gully Boulder

I

H

Behemoth 1

Suspicion Stone

Illness Spires

big!

Behemoth 2

G

Bitch's Brew

E

D

to F

ridgeline

C

B

A. Mystery Achievement
B. Mavericks
C. Bob Is a Man
D. Redline Boulder
E. Hateful Traverse
F. Poker Face
G. Illness Area
H. Giant Steps
I. Fluffy Bunny
J. Aspen Grove Boulder
K. Banjo Boulder
L. Manifest Destiny Area

6

A

Little Cupcake

old road

mile marker 268.00

Golden →

CLEAR CREEK CANYON GULLY 268

"There's bouldering in Clear Creek? You've got to be fucking kidding me!" Though this highly-traveled canyon has become a semi-tolerable sport climbing area over the last decade, it wasn't until hyper-motivated college professor and diaper-changer Greg Johnson took a look in one of the canyon's rugged lower gullies that any bouldering was found.

The rock, a metamorphic gneiss, ranges from sublimely solid to appallingly loose along the length of the canyon. Fortunately, the milling action of the small stream in Gully 268 has endowed these boulders with a smooth, solid veneer, much like the rock on nearby Anarchy Wall.

Once up bouldering in Gully 268 you'll quickly forget the traffic, smut and noise of Route 6 below, where countless busloads of dead-end white trash are shuttled up to cookie-cutter casinos in Black Hawk and Central City. Expect lots of highballs ... and don't bother showing up during the warmer months—unless your idea of a good time is total sun exposure on a hot, overgrown hillside and sliding off of greasy slopers. This is a perfect winter area, even during the coldest months, melting out as quickly as Morrison and holding sun for most of the day.

A. Mystery Achievement
B. Mavericks
C. Bob is a Man
D. Redline Boulder
E. Hateful Traverse
F. The Poker Face (out of view)
G. The Illness Area
H. Giant Steps
I. The Fluffy Bunny Bouldering
J. The Aspen Grove Boulder
K. The Banjo Boulder

Directions: Drive 3.6 miles up Clear Creek Canyon (US 6 west out of Golden) to a large pull-out on the left (south) side of the road before a road cut. This pull-out is at mile marker 268.00. Walk east out of the parking lot to the tunnel under the road. The tunnel drops you off at the base of the gully where the bouldering is found.

A. MYSTERY ACHIEVEMENT AREA

Though the road noise is a bit oppressive, the stone is nice and you can warm up well for the thuggier problems at Mavericks. Climb a sliding dirt chute on the right, 100 feet past the tunnel, onto the bench below these boulders.

MYSTERY ACHIEVEMENT BOULDER

The big boulder on your right once atop the chute. The landing presents an exemplary model of erosion control! Let us praise those ancient stone-workers who built their home beneath the boulder.

Mystery Achievement   Little Cupcake

1. The Spooky Spanker V5 *

Yikes! Start with your right hand on an under-cling then slap your way up into the thin crack and rounded prominence above.

2. Mystery Achievement V3 ***

Climb the proud face over the center of the platform, aiming for the rounded crack up high. If you blow the exit you'll pitch past the platform.

THE LITTLE CUPCAKE

This diminutive, though fun, block sits just behind and east of Mystery Achievement. It's a good place to warm-up, especially if you milk the traverse for a lap or two.

1. Leftinski V0

Climb the small bulge on the left side of the boulder.

2. Slopeski V3 *

Climb past slopers in the center of the boulder onto the rounded ramp above.

3. Rightinski V1

Fumble your way past slots up the right end of the wall.

4. Traverski V2 *

Monkey swing left across good holds on the lower part of the wall, doing your best to keep your feet out of the dirt.

THE NUISANCE BOULDER

This is the low, flat-topped boulder on the left 50 feet up the trail from Mystery Achievement. The problems climb the bulging, surprisingly slopey west face.

1. Left V3
Climb thin holds on the left side of the face to the baby's-bottom top-out.

2. Right V3
The line just right of the groove.

3. Full V5 *
From jugs on the south face traverse lip and finish on #2.

B. MAVERICKS

The premier boulder in the gully, boasting a handful of superb lines on perfect rock as well as a few stimulating "moderates." Continue three minutes up the gully from Mystery Achievemt to get here.

1. North Shore V9 ***
Begin on sloping pods down and left of the Mavericks corner and bust a huge move up to a sloping horizontal, then finish on Mavericks.

2. The Plunge V4
Mountaineer up onto the block left of #3. Pinch a rounded hole with the left hand and reach out into the crack. Spooky!

3. Mavericks V5 ****
Simply brilliant. Start low under the hanging arete with your right hand in a good mailbox slot. Slap moves take you to a lip "moment." The Two Jack Start (V6 ***) begins at the good right-hand hand jam below #4 and traverses the diagonaling crack leftwards into Mavericks.

4. Dry Dock V2 *
Scary as shit. Start atop the block and move right to the lip, then bust a scummy mantle over the worst landing.

5. Joe's Dyno V? **
Move from the crack to the big, sloping bump. Yank on it (left hand) and fire to the lip.

6. Tube Direct V7
Sds four feet right with your hands in sloper jams. Crimp up the face to the crack feature above you. Jingus yet pointless.

7. The Tube V3 *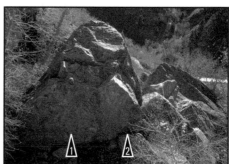
Sds on the southwest arete, ramp left along the lip until you hit the diagonaling crack, undercling it and bust over the lip. Harder if you take the crack hold as a finger lock.

8. Shore Break V3 *
Sds low and left on the southwest prow over the blocks, your left hand on an incut flake. Bust right along sloping ramps until you hit the top of #7.

9. 41st Street V7 ***
The plumb line on the triangular south face. Start in the underclings at chest height then do what must be done to gain the top. Powerful and classic.

Greg Johnson on Mavericks
photo: Josh Deuto

C. Bob is a Man Rock
This aesthetic little block is 50 feet up the gully from Mavericks, just above the white-wash. Swirly, man.

1. Bob is a Man V4 **
Step up onto a block below the middle of the northwest face then grapple past crimps to gain the lip.

2. V2
Sds on the under the southwest arete then surf along its length to the top.

D. The Redline Boulder
This pointy, isolated block offers some of the better moderates in the area on grippy, brown and red stone (though the sloping landing leaves something to be desired). Traverse down and right across the gully just 3-5 minutes uphill from Mavericks (this is the start of the trail out to the Poker Face). The boulder is 50 feet east of the gully on a bench.

1. Bulge I V1
Climb the leftmost line on the southwest face then amble up the big slab above. Start with your right hand on a cracked flake.

2. Bulge II V2
Begin four feet right of #1 and climb the rough, crystalline groove feature to the slab.

3. The Red Line V3 **
This semi-classic follows the obvious clean dihedral to the crack traverse. Easier up high.

4. Thin Red Line V5 **
Sds on crimpers on the southeast arete (just right of the dihedral) and climb into the finger traverse crack above, which you follow 10 feet right to finish on #5.

5. Red V2 **
Step off the boulder against the east face and yard on the good crack holds to a distant jug/ledge and then the lip. Thuggy.

6. North Slabs *
Fun problems and variations in the V0-V1 range can be done on the licheny north face.

E. HATEFUL TRAVERSE WALL (NOT PICTURED)
Named such because no one seems to like it, except the pud-yanking loser who put up all the problems. This red-and-beige wall sits just right of the black-streaked waterfall and forms the base of a large cliff approximately 100 feet uphill from the Redline Boulder.

1. Hateful Traverse V5 *
Begin left (just right of the perennially wet black streak) and move right across the horizontal crack onto the face. Head up into the obvious break via #3, just left of a glassy bulge.

2. Hateful Downclimb V1 *
The easiest way on, and off the wall. Climb slots up the arete-feature on the left end of the wall.

3. Hateful Upclimb V3 *
Sds below the end of the traverse and climb up either past the flake or into the groove, eventually topping out over a second bulge. Many variations possible.

F. THE POKER FACE
This boulder sits well out of the gully on the hillside, more or less level with the Illness Boulders and 150 yards east (down canyon). The offerings here range from dynamic bulges on impeccable stone to a long, powerful traverse of the diagonal crack line on the south face.
Approach time: 10 minutes.

1. Trundle of Love V6 **
The fun problem six feet right of the wall's left margin. Ass low, crimp your way off the rail and up the bulge. V2 from the stand.

2. Texas Hold'Em V9/10 ***
Start sitting down on #1 and follow the diagonal crack system up and right across the boulder, topping out where the crack ends on the east face. Feature climbing at its finest. This problem is much easier if you start further right.

3. Chucky Cheese V7 **
Start four feet right of #1 with your right hand in a good pocket. Heel hook left and reef up to a good inset, then huck high and right to finish. Much easier (V3) if you move left from the inset.

4. Bulge V2 *
Start on good jugs over the large block and move out and left into the bulge on nice, grippy stone.

5. Low Seam V6 **
This problem can be done either as a sds to the crack or taken a little further right for full difficulty. Sds three feet right of the block on a good jug and work right along the seam to its end, eventually hitting a crimp out right and throwing back into the crack to finish.

6. Wretch Like Me V3 *
Climb out the cave onto the dark rock of the east face, starting with your left hand on a sloper in the obvious V-notch below the lip and your right on a low crimper.

7. Calipula V4 *
Start on #6 but traverse right just below the lip, off-routing the jugs up and over. Hit the arete on the right and climb the thin face above, off-routing the arete for the left hand.

G. THE ILLNESS AREA

This sunny zone is 10 steep minutes up the gully from Mavericks and has yielded the highest density of problems in the gully. These blocks are scattered on the hillside just east of the gully below the large crag, which is easily distinguished by a smiling blue face spray-painted on the rock. Head straight up the hill above the Redline Boulder on a trail that takes you past the RSV Cave and the Bitch's Brew Boulder before traversing back left to the Illness proper.
Approach time: 10 minutes

RSV Cave

What it lacks in stature this wall more than makes up for in terms of steeps. This west-facing cave is perched on the hillside about 100 feet up and east from The Hateful Traverse Wall.

1. V V4*
Sds start hyper-low on the left side of the cave, your hands on a sloping rail. Move right up the prow on bizarro holds.

2. S V2 *
The center line. Sds on a good, incut flake then press out the lip.

3. R V4 **
Low-start in the very back of the rightmost part of the cave then twist your way lipwards into the dihedral. Thuggy. RSV (V5) climbs R to the lip before traversing left across S to finish on V.

Bitch's Brew Boulder

Just up and right from RSV, this giant boulder has a proud problem waiting to be done on the deadly southeast overhang. Though a handful of crummy lines have been done over the eroding dirt hillside on the boulder's northwest face, the real gems climb the southwest face.

1. Arete V2 *
Climb the funky, hanging prow on the southwest corner of the boulder.

2. Scoop V3 *
This line takes the pegmatite scoop right of the prow.

3. Bitch's Brew V7 **
Powerful and fussy. Sds with your left on a crimp in the peg band and your right higher on a flat hold, then slap your way up the bulging face above the slab-slapper landing.

Illness Boulders

Traverse left from the top of Bitch's Brew to get here (one minute). Two radically undercut blocks with perfect, flat landings and lots of sun make this one of the choicest zones on the hillside.

Left Illness

This is the higher, pointy block to the west. The recently-completed cave problem facing the gully offers the promise of double-digit sickness and elite four-star athleticism.

1. Squid V8 **

Start on the south face, just left of the hanging prow, with your left hand on a pinch and your right hand on a crimp. Reel right past slopers around the corner then traverse right along the low seam, off-routing the upper jug rail. V4 if you use the jug rail.

2. Battling Seizure Robots V5 **

Do the easy variation on #1 then dice your way past sloping crimpers on the gold face/prow just left of #3. Have your spotter stand below the pads so you don't go off the 100-foot cliff.

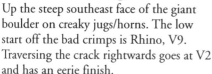

3. Dead Lizard V1 ***

Up the steep southeast face of the giant boulder on creaky jugs/horns. The low start off the bad crimps is Rhino, V9. Traversing the crack rightwards goes at V2 and has an eerie finish.

RIGHT ILLNESS

This is the roof/boulder perched on the east side of the grotto.

4. Squeeze Job V3

A useless little campus move up the wall left of the choss heap at the base of the block.

5. Heaping Helping V2 *

Ascend the heap, make a long stretch for a jug over the lip of the boulder and press it out.

Note: Problems #6, #7 and #8 share a common sds on the right with your hands matched in a good, low horizontal.

6. Bacterial V5 **

Thuggy and acrobatic. Head up and left along the lip on inset seams, off-routing the jugs to the right. Turn the lip on good holds right of the heap.

7. Viral V3 *

Lock off and stretch right for jugs from the sds.

8. Ebola V7 **

The integral lip traverse, crossing #6, #7 and #8 to finish with an exit crux on the far left (north) end of the boulder over the jingus landing. Potent.

Illness Spires

These two massive, pointy blocks abut each other just on the bench just uphill and east of the Illness Boulders and offer some great warm-ups.

Left Spire

1. Sport Park is Neither V2 **

Climb the left line, directly below the prominent arete. Either bail right into the bowl or finish on the 40-foot arete (5.9+).

2. Puss in Boots V3 *

This line starts on low underclings then fires past fragile crimpers on the brown face four feet right of #1. Elegant.

3. The Skirted Snail V4 *

Slap your way up the rounded prow on the southwest corner of the boulder. Slabby.

4. The Downclimb V0+

This is the best way off for #1-3. It follows the seams in the black streak on the south face of the boulder, just right of #3.

Right Spire

5. High Slab V0+ **

A beautiful line on positive edges up the middle of the high slab just right of the chimney. Good, heady bouldering.

H. Giant Steps

This is the jumble of enormous boulders 50 yards uphill and north from the Illness Area. Many proud, high (20+ feet) lines have been done on these austere brown rocks, yet the hardest lines have yet to cede. Bring at least three crash pads or you're unlikely to leave the ground. This zone is more-or-less directly below the big crag with the blue smiley face and holds sun most of the day in the winter.
Approach time: 15 minutes.

Suspicion Stone (not pictured)

This easy-to-spot, south-facing overhang is left (west of the gully) on the small bench across from and slightly uphill of the Illness Area.

1. Nietzche V3

The leftmost line, on funky flakes and holds into the groove.

2. Marx V3 *

The tall center line, which more or less follows the rib/prow. Eastwood (V6), tackles the face right of the prow, off-routing the prow for the left hand.

3. Freud V1
The rightmost problem up the featured but dirty groove.

GULLY BOULDER
The sds to the one problem here will be horrendously hard. The rock is perfect—polished to an alarmingly slick sheen by the milling action of water and covered in grey and white swirls. This boulder is in the wash, level with Giant Steps Left and just below the big slab in the gully.

1. The Italian Stallion V5 ****
Start low and left on a sloping jug and work right
across the horizontal until you can punch straight out the slippery prow. Simply brilliant!

H. GIANT STEPS

GIANT STEPS LEFT
This is the left of the two huge blocks that faces almost due west. The problems are high and the footholds still slightly friable, but the landings are for the most part flat. This wall holds sun most of the day in the winter.

NORTH FACE
1. Slaves of Truth V1 *
This fine pocket climb takes the inside face around the corner and uphill from the arete.

2. Masters of Irony V3 *
Begin on #1 but work your way up the rounded prow just right via underclings and slopers.

WEST FACE
3. Speed Zoo V4 **
Begin just right of the arete on high underclings. Punch straight up the wall above, past another undercling and right-hand sidepull to a crimpy finish.

4. The Moose V4 **
Begin on #3 and continue right on good underclings (or climb directly into these on plate-crimpers), bust for a left-hand sloper, and fire high and right to a made-to-order handlebar jug. Tall and classic.

5. Undone I V? **
The line up the center of the wall over the rectangular block. Groovy.

6. Undone II V? ****
The very distinct rightmost line on the wall, following a vein of quartz up a black streak.

GIANT STEPS RIGHT

This is the rightmost of the two blocks, easily distinguished by an aesthetic prow on its right end, just north of a huge, dead tree. The landings are a bit worse here, despite efforts to shore up the eroding hillside.

1. Headbanger's Ball V6 *

Ouch! This short but fierce problem tackles the bulging wall left of the black-stained dihedral on the wall's uphill end. Start with your ass in the dirt!

2. Star Drive V0 *

Climb the corner, taking care with mossy footholds. Check out the mank bolt on top!

3. Rolly-Polly V5 **

Though the first move is the hardest, this line ain't over 'til it's over. Begin on a good right-hand crimp six feet right of the dihedral and fire up to the sloping horizontal, then trend right and up to finish.

4. La Fissura V1 *

Climb out the obvious right-leaning dihedral in the middle of the wall over the shite-ous block landing.

5. Il Precario V6 **

"Precarious" in Italian. Climb the face right of the crack, aiming for a juggy seam up high and right. Crimpy and committing on psychedelic, swirly rock.

6. Up with People V4 ***

Climb the prow, starting on good holds at head height and firing high and right for a sloper before wrapping back left around the arete. Aren't people great?

7. Down with People V6 **

This link-up combines a low (read: groundhog) traverse of the southwest cave behind the dead tree with #6. Needless to say, the prow is much scarier when you're pumped.

I. THE FLUFFY BUNNY BOULDERING

Sixty feet straight up the gully from Giant Steps (at the top of the whitewash) sit these deceptively steep and polished chunks of bullet rock. Though seemingly "downright lame," the left wall of the alcove is completely devoid of texture, especially on the top-outs, making for some hilarious beached-whale maneuvering.

FLUFFY BOULDER

The squatty, slopey, and south-facing left wall of the alcove above the nice, grassy landings.

1. Smooth Operator V2 **
Climb the rippled face past horizontals to finish on glass.

2. Scrumpy V0+ *
The dihedral/seam up the middle of the wall.

3. Frumpy V2 **
The rightmost line up the glassy bulge. Harder if you off-route the rounded three-finger pocket and anything right of that.

BUNNY BOULDER

The overhanging, right wall of the alcove. Featured with jugs, crimps and horns, this little gem climbs quite steeply and powerfully on surprisingly bomber stone. Bring a spotter for the rightmost problems, which hang out over a nasty mini-couloir.

4. Fuzzy Bunny V2 **
Sds on good incuts then fire up the polished face above. One variation powers into the jug undercling up and right.

5. Blood Bunny V4 **
Sds on a good right-hand layaway and left-hand pinch, then power on and slap your way up the prow/rib feature to the top of the wall.

6. Funny Bunny V3 * ⬤
Sds with your hands in a good crack down and right of the rib, then work your way up the juggy groove above on good flakes.

7. Bunny's Traverse V6 **
Powerful and harder than it looks. Traverse the wall from right to left, dropping in from the jug/horns on #5 to a pair of flakes that lead into #4. Add a V-grade if you off-route these horns.

J. THE ASPEN GROVE BOULDER

Climb the whitewash immediately above the Giant Steps and follow the gully northeast. Find this large, pleasant boulder 30 yards up from the top of the whitewash. There is plenty of potential for new problems in and around the grove.
Approach time: 20 minutes.

1. V4 * ⬤

The leftmost line, on wavy rock directly above the large pit. Undercling low and left then punch past slopers to the lip. Tricky.

2. Center V3 *

Climb this pretty little line by kneel-starting with your left hand on a gray edge and your right hand on a crimp, six feet right of #1.

3. Right V2

Take the aforementioned crimp with your left hand and move right to a layback, then up.

K. THE BANJO BOULDER

Despite the long, arduous approach, this mobile-home sized slab of good, gray stone 30 minutes uphill from the car is worth a visit. The wall offers everything from thuggy cave problems to testy vertical face climbs, with plenty of highball top-outs to keep things spicy. Its idyllic setting in a grassy meadow bisected by a small stream makes for a fun hang in the warmer months. To get here, hike out of the gully onto its right (east) side above the Aspen Grove Boulder then contour back left into the gully across from an attractive, multi-tiered crag to the west. Beware the sketch hobo encampment.
Approach time: 30 minutes.

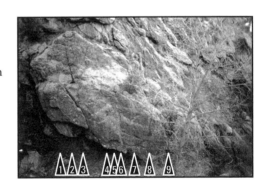

1. Undone ***

The highball arete-to-face line starting on the north arete of the wall and turning a terrifying roof at 13 feet.

2. Eric's Highball V3 * ⬤

Cruise up the crack to the roof, move left, then up and over on knobular holds via a committing rock-over.

3. Dihedral V0+ ** ⬤

The obvious crack/dihedral splitting the wall.

NOTE: #4-7 all begin on the right side of the cave, sitting down with your hands on a large horn and moving left into underclings.

4. Traverse V7 *

From the sds cross the entirety of the cave until you can move out on the layaways of #5 and backhand left into the crack at seven feet. Either climb the crack to finish or drop off.

5. Sandcastle (aka The Coveted Double Bird Toe) V8 **

Every thug's wet dream. Stay low across the cave until you hit the sloper/corner system on the left side. Head out the slopes to a painful vertical slot over the lip, slap right to a beach-ball, then fire up to a diagonaling finger slot. The good holds out right over the lip on #6 are off. Finish out on the crack.

6. Banjos V6 ***

Work left through the cave to the last good undercling, then climb straight out onto the lip and head for the diagonaling finger slot. Finish via the crack. Roofy, sustained and perplexing.

7. Rufus's Wonder Move V4 ** 😀

Go left five feet from the horn, grab crimps over the lip, and stand up right into a flake/groove system. Technical and strange.

8. Courtesy V2 * 😀

The high problem up the center of the vertical wall, aiming for a finger slot at 12 feet.

9. Sympathy V3 **

The slanting finger crack on the right side of the wall, eight feet left of a trough with a bush. Finish by staying left on flakes or punching right to a horn at the top of the crack.

L. MANIFEST DESTINY AREA

"Go West, young man!" Perched high on the hillside in the faint gully 200 yards west of the main area, this collection of bigger-than-they-look-from-below boulders offers the superlative Manifest Destiny boulder and two barely-touched behemoths just downhill. Be careful not to dislodge any rocks from here, as they may very well tumble all the way down to the road!

Directions: Either hike directly up the ridge west of the gully from the parking area via a faint climber's trail or approach from the gully itself via a trail cutting west from Giant Steps across the base of the large crag. Manifest Destiny is another 100 yards up the hill once you hit the ridge and can be distinguished by the large dead pine tree just below its southwest face. The Behemoth Boulders are just two minutes downhill from here.

MANIFEST DESTINY

The main draw, offering over a dozen steep, deceptively hard problems on interesting, black-and gray-streaked stone as well as good views of the canyon and the jerky-selling weirdo in the large pull-out directly below. Much walking.

1. Traverse of Bliss to Arete of Piss V4 **

A long name for a long problem. Leftward traverse the obvious horizontal on the northwest face, finishing out on the tricky arete all the way uphill.

2. Slab Oneski V1
The leftmost slab problem on the face via small edges, just uphill from the rock-pile landing.

3. Slab Twoski V1
From good holds near the start of the traverse, rock up past crimps to good holds on the slab.

4. Josh's Roof V8 *
Awkward and difficult. Climb the roof six feet right of the start of the traverse. Full V8 rating assumes you start with your hands under the lip on the crimp and the undercling, bro.

5. THC Engineering V6 **
The engaging prow just over the Nepalese rice-paddy terrace. Start low on the flake, slap up and right to a jug then reel back left on crimpers to gain the crack above.

6. Mangina Crack V?
The obvious, not-too-hard-looking crack on the south/southwest face of the boulder, just above the huge dead tree. To fall is to be impaled.

7. Jade's Variation V3 *
Climb the crack to mid-height, then bust right onto the headwall through good holds.

8. Flaps V6 ***
The classic face line up the bulging black wall six feet right of the crack. Catch the finger lock at mid-height with your right hand and finish via a committing lunge to a horn.

9. Kilgore V6 ***
A dynamic excursion on underclings and sidepulls just four feet right of #8. Snag the finger lock with your left hand and finish just left of the large groove.

10. Cephalic Index V7 ***
The prominent nose on the boulder's south face, starting left below the spiny bush. Roll through from the honking-huge sidepull jug to a phat pinch, then slap your way up the rounded prow.

12. Divine Right V5 *
Start on the double underclings at head height then paw your way through the overlaps, eventually moving left into the crack.

13. Prowling V8 **
The long prow on the southeast side of boulder, right of a small tree. Start low, just right of the tree, and move up and right on poor crimps, eventually finishing out on #15.

14. Rape V3 *
Climb the groove from an undercling halfway up the prow. Rape and Pillage (V4) starts on this problem and links into #15.

15. Pillage V1
Start at a good hold on the steep face and pull for the lip jug.

THE FIN

This tiny blade of rock 15 feet east of Manifest Destiny offers three short but fun problems.

1. Two-Timing with Jocasta V1
Layback the steep left prow of the rock.

2. Jade's Line V5 **
Start on the low jug on the left and slap your way up the overhang without using the prow.

3. Philoctetes V3 *
The funky, powerful seam up the middle of the face.

BEHEMOTH II

Big as a house and (mostly) blank as shit, this hard-to-miss chunk of gray stone sits in the faint gully about 70 yards below Manifest Destiny.

1. Creaky Flake V0+ *
The thuggy, juggy romp on the obvious flake splitting the west face. Use caution on the blocky top-out.

2. Mr. Bitchy V6 ****🎯

Sds on the pink quartz horn then battle up the scenic arete at the junction of the massive south face and the more manageable west face. Super-steep and super-highball. Climb near the crystalline crack on the left to finish (the prow proper, out right, is unclimbed).

BEHEMOTH I

Why does this boulder only look five feet tall from the highway? A few problems have been done on the low, wavy southeast face, but the proud line out the left side of the south face needs to be done in a big way. This boulder is directly downhill from Behemoth II.

CLEAR CREEK ALSO-RANS

Not surprisingly, this craggy canyon offers other bouldering possibilities as well. These areas suffer two major drawbacks, however. They are either so close to the road as to be completely noisome and annoying, or they sit in the creek and are inaccessible during high water—or both. Nevertheless, for the bored boulderer looking for something different or for those who just can't get enough of the tranquil, pristine ambience of the canyon, We've listed a few choicer areas below. Don't forget to bring hip waders and earplugs!

MILE MARKER 270.00

Look for this mile marker 1.6 miles up the canyon and park where you can (there's a small pull-out on the left just before the mile marker). These boulders are on an elevated bench on the right (north) side of the canyon and can be reached via a steep scramble along the road-cut. Not much else is known.

MILE MARKER 269.50

Look for this mile marker 2.7 miles up the canyon and park in an ample pull-out on the left where a large, white cross reading "Brandy" commemorates a tragic car accident. On the other (south) side of the creek find a smooth, left-leaning, overhanging arete (V4 ***), accessible only when the creek is frozen.

NEW RIVER WALL

This is the obvious, streamside cliff band 6.1 miles up the canyon on the right and is home to the classic, overhanging corner of Sonic Youth. Park where you (safely) can, make your way up-canyon to Tunnel 2 and cross north, walking back down-canyon roughly 150 yards to reach the base of the wall. A small, streamside cave just west of Sonic Youth provides for thuggy variations on positive rock, with the possibility for highball top-outs.

ANARCHY WALL BOULDERING

Drive 6.8 miles up the Canyon, parking on the left just after you pass through Tunnel 3. A small cluster of solid, featured blocks has tumbled down the hill from the Anarchy Wall above. The twin slabs at the bottom are a great place to teach beginning climbers.

THE WAVE WALL

This varnished piece of bullet granite is only accessible during the colder months, unless your idea of a landing is three feet of icy, swiftly-moving water!
Drive 11.5 miles up the canyon, taking a left onto US 6 at the stoplight which marks the junction with Highway 119. The Primo Wall will be on your right after Tunnel 6, 1.2 miles from the stoplight; the Wave Wall is at 1.4 miles, just upstream. The Wave Wall is the polished, concave golden wall forming a sort of mini-alcove right above the river. Park where you can and ford across. Though not exceptionally hard, the problems here are quiet aesthetic.

THE DIKE WALL

This sunny traverse wall is 1.6 miles above the stoplight at the junction of US 6 and Hwy 119. It is just above Hwy 6 to the right (north), directly across from an old, reddish, abandoned building on the south side of the creek. The traverse starts on the left at an undercling and moves right along the sloping ripples. There is also potential for a few up-problems.

MATTHEWS-WINTERS PARK

Mike Hickey, North Face Millennium   photo: Greg Johnson

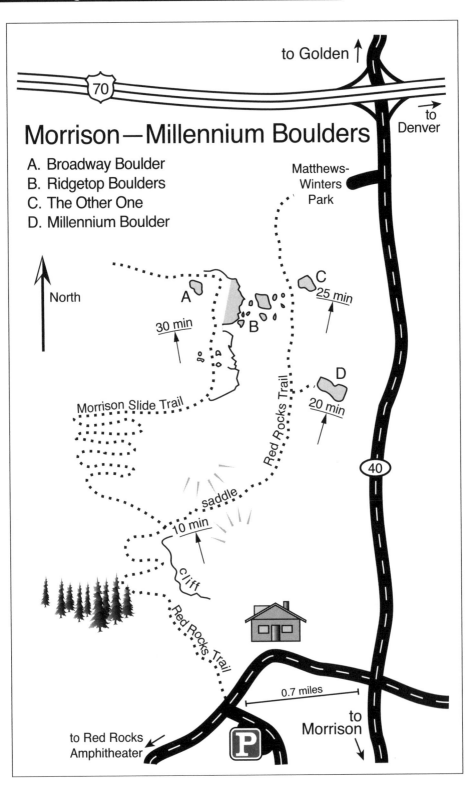

to Golden ↑

to Denver →

70

Morrison—Millennium Boulders

A. Broadway Boulder
B. Ridgetop Boulders
C. The Other One
D. Millennium Boulder

Matthews-
Winters
Park

North ↑

C
25 min

A

30 min

B

D
20 min

Morrison Slide Trail

Red Rocks Trail

40

saddle

10 min

cliff

Red Rocks Trail

0.7 miles

to Morrison

to Red Rocks Amphitheater

P

MATTHEWS-WINTERS PARK
(THE MILLENNIUM BOULDER)

With the "Bouldering Mecca" of Morrison close by, who would a thunk? Peaceful and pristine despite its situation at the edge of the Denver city limits, this area offers the choice Millennium Boulder, a species of sandstone erratic, as well as a concentration of good bouldering on the hillside and plateau just west. The three-star problems on the Millennium are "must-dos" for their grades, but don't just stop there. The Ridgetop Area offers great traverses as well as the difficult highball The Holdout, taller and scarier than many of the problems done so far on the north side of the Millennium. This place is a great alternative to the slime and spray of Morrison.

Directions: From the junction of Highway 93 and Highway 6 (to Clear Creek Canyon) continue south on Highway 6 for 2.3 miles and take a right on Heritage Road. Go 0.9 miles past three stoplights to a junction with Highway 40, where you take a right onto 40 west. Continue south on 40 another 2.7 miles, passing under I-70 at 1.2 miles and the entrance to Matthews/Winters Park at 1.6 miles. Turn right into Red Rocks Park and Amphitheater and drive west 0.7 miles to a gate. This is the northern entrance to Red Rocks. Turn left just before the gate into a small dirt parking lot and park.

Annette Bunge on the Millennium   photo: Greg Johnson

THE RIDGETOP BOULDERS

Directions: From the parking area head north on the Red Rocks Trail for roughly 10-12 minutes, passing a large pink wall on the right and working your way up switchbacks before arriving at a T-junction. Head left (west) on the Morrison Slide Trail past seven steep switchbacks until you hit a high, scenic plateau with great views of Denver (approximately 25 minutes). Walk north along the plateau, passing a clump of low, red boulders. Approximately 175 yards past these boulders notice a faint draw on the right (east) leading through the cliff band. The Ridgetop Boulders are just north of this draw; the Hillside Boulders are strung out along the slope leading down to the Other One.

For the Broadway Boulder, continue on another minute until the trail bends west. Go west 50 yards. The boulder is in the trees, 75 feet off the trail to the south.

Approach Time: 25-30 minutes.

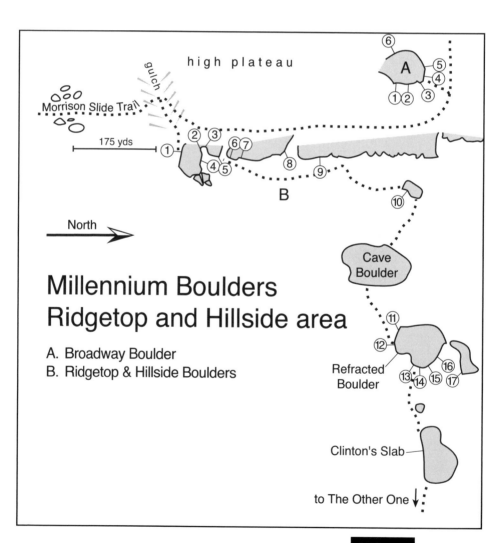

Millennium Boulders
Ridgetop and Hillside area

A. Broadway Boulder
B. Ridgetop & Hillside Boulders

A. Broadway Boulder

This isolated block, nestled in a pretty forest of scrubby pines, offers fun crimper problems on quality stone and a handful of good moderates. Wedge-shaped and slightly gritty, this block is reminiscent of the good stuff up at Flagstaff Mountain.

1. V3 *
Start in funky pockets six feet right of the tree and diagonal right and up.

2. V3 *
Start in the good horizontal and cruise up the face past flakes and edges.

3. Marcelo's Madness V7 **
A continuous, crimpy traverse on perfect dark stone. Sds at the northeast corner of the boulder on a rail at knee-height, heading left through a tricky crux to finish on #1. Named for Marcelo's proud winger off the Broadway Brewing Building in Denver.

4. V0 * 🐾**
The fun green/black slab on the north side of the boulder. Start low on a good horn and amble up the dinner plates. The arete to the left is also V0.

5. V0+ * 🐾
A slightly harder version of #4 beginning just to the right. Fun!

6. V4
A crimpy traverse beginning on the horn and working right on the steeper, low part of the wall, finishing out along the west face at big holes in the horizontal. Sharp.

B. Ridgetop Boulders

With the highest concentration of problems along the ridgetop, this intriguing and varied area is worth the hike. The rock is a strange, red sandstone littered with sinker pockets and tiny crimps. The views of the hogback across the road and on into Denver are stunning. Some of the landings tend to slope, so bring a crash pad or two.

The Holdout Boulder

This is the big boulder with the intimidating dark north face, jutting out from the ridgeline.

1. V2
Move up the south face on slightly friable crimps and dishes above the rocky landing. Will clean up well.

2. V5 *
Start on the uphill side of the boulder and hand traverse left along the horizontal seam. Strenuous.

3. The Holdout V8 **

The stunning line on the north face, straight up the black streak, on solid red stone. Either start on waist-high crimps and crank high to a shallow three-finger pocket, or sds in the little cave for The Full Holdout, V9 ***.

FUCK PLATO BOULDER

The small wall just north of The Holdout with a prominent arete on the right side.

4. V2

Step right onto a small ledge then crimp your way up the dark green stone.

5. Fuck Plato V4 *

Named in honor of professor Greg Johnson's favorite Greek philosopher/pederast. Sds on the arete then work past pebbles and crimpers to a sketch-mo top-out. Harder and steeper than it looks.

THE PERCH

The wall just north again, right of the dirty crack system.

6. Choss One V0+

Grainy and kinda loose. Start with your left hand in a good basketball-sized hueco on the arete, then up.

7. Choss Two V2

Sds. Work over the bulge on loose flakes, passing a good mouth-shaped pocket.

8. The Perch V5 **

The poor-man's Dogmatics. Sds this elegant rig low and left (east) under a small cave, then angle up and right across the red, green and black-streaked face to finish at a large white crystal on a ramp. Continuous.

THE PORCH

Just across the little gully from The Perch find this long wall with striking black and white-streaked rock.

9. Donkey Traverse V6 **

This 48-foot pumpfest has it all, from slopers to tiny pockets to incut rails. Begin far right (north) on the wall at an obvious incut jug and work left, staying low around the corner and finishing up past thin moves in a large hole on the south face. Not to be confused with its more worthless cousin, The Monkey Traverse, at Flagstaff.

The Porch-left

THE TICKET

This curious little cave/scoop feature is 100 yards north of the main area just below a prominent prow on the cliff line. Also known as the "World's Shortest Highball."

The Porch-right

10. The Ticket V6 *

Sds on double underclings and pimp out the seam to the lip of the cave. Powerful and frustrating.

HILLSIDE BOULDERS

These boulders can either be approached by dropping down from the Ridgetop Boulders or by walking uphill from the Other One. They offer a smattering of pleasant middle-grade problems as well as some easier slabs for beginners.

The Ticket

THE REFRACTED BOULDER

A good, sunny block with technical problems from V1 to V5 on friendly red stone. It's about 200 feet downhill from The Ticket, directly below and north of an enormous boulder with an east-facing choss cave.

11. Suburban Skyline V1 *

Layback the ramp on the left (west) side of the south face. Dirty but fun.

12. Thin Face V5 *

Start on crimps in the funky white scoops then move left onto the red face. Technical.

13. Pain V6

The horrible meat-grinder crack on the east prow of the boulder. Sds in the gnarly bushes. Utterly worthless.

14. V2 *

Up the finger crack/seam on the prow just right of #3.

15. Monomaniac V5 *

Climb the aesthetic red face via a tips mono and strange gastons. The crack on the right is off. Tendon injury potential.

16. Refracted V4 **
The excellent finger crack up the face right of #5. Slopey, devious, technical.

17. Fearful Symmetry V3 *
Locate this fun little problem up a faint corner on the boulder just north. Sds, top out left on nubbins.

THE CLINTON BOULDER
Downhill another 60 yards is this big slabby blob with V0 problems up its flanks.

THE MILLENNIUM BOULDER AND THE OTHER ONE

Directions: At the T-junction take a right (east), continuing along the Red Rocks Trail over a small saddle. Continue north along the trail into an open, grassy area. 3-4 minutes along the trail you'll see the enormous Millennium Boulder in the meadow down and right. The Other One is another 300 yards along the trail, 80 feet downhill and to the east.

C. THE OTHER ONE
If it's not the Millennium Boulder than it must be that other one! Though not as compact or aesthetic as the Millennium, The Other One is a great place to warm up or cool down after your session. Though most of the problems are moderate, one vicious V9 and a couple of testy highballs should keep even the "hardest" of the "hard" awake.

SOUTHWEST SIDE

1. V0+
Start on the far left (west) end of the boulder and traverse eight feet right on flakes.

2. Vee-Wonderful V1
Grab a good hueco with your left hand and pull over the bulge.

3. Other One Dyno V2 *
Huck to a good jug/flake from the finger slots on the left end of the horizontal.

4. Angel V3 **
Honor student by day, hooker by night. With your right hand, undercling a bomber cobble in a hole then head left to the slopey horizontal and up.

5 . Little Wing V3 ✶✶

A higher, more continuous version of #4. Start above the rocky landing in sloping holes then realm up past a nipple hold to good crimps.

6. Voodoo Child V5 ✶✶

Sds on a horn just left of the nose of the boulder and punch up to a good hole. Surmount the double bulges straight up for full value or bail right below the crux finish if your underwear needs changing.

7. V6

Sds right under the nose, snag the hole over the lip with your left, and fire high and right to a crumbling edge. Real bad.

NORTH SIDE

8. Black Fly V9 ✶✶

A real tendon test for pocket aficionados. Start on sloping crimps under the tallest part of the north face then yank past two small, sharp pockets to the lip. Ouch!

9. Mike's Muscle Car V4 ✶

Vroom, vroom! Sds in a crumbly horizontal behind the trees, crank left and up then reel left along the crispy horizontal, topping out on #8. Gymnastic and pumpy. The straight-up is V4 as well.

10. Buttercups V2

Start in the horizontal but move right past an obvious pebble, topping out in good but dirty holes 10 feet right.

D. THE MILLENNIUM BOULDER

Strangely overlooked for years by the Morrison crew, who proclaimed it to be either "too blank" or "too chossy," this geologic anomaly didn't begin to see serious development until Greg Johnson and Bob Williams visited in 1998 for another look. A chunk of bullet, Eldorado Canyon sandstone swallowed by the Earth and spat back up 30 miles to the south, this 16-foot high block embedded in a grassy meadow is nothing short of stellar, especially for highball and thin pocket aficionados.

SOUTH AND EAST FACES

1. Warm-up Ledges V0-V3

The short, upper end of the south face has a myriad of warm-up possibilities.

2. B.C. V2 *
Start on the southeast face where it turns vertical. Pull on via big slopers then head up the glassy rock.

3. Cargo Cult V3 **
Start on a horizontal pinch, move right to a sidepull, pass a pocket and rocket to the lip.

4. Epiphany V5 **
The technical southeast prow of the rock. Match the sloper, then heel hook past a dish to finish on deep pockets. Starting here and finishing by traversing into #2 is Chef's Mangoes (V6).

5. Deseret V2 *
Six feet right of #4 locate this mini-buttress with a white-stained flake. V6 with the sds. Funky.

6. Cannibal Dance V7 *
Follow the thin, right-leaning seam to a shallow pocket left of the seam in black rock.

7. Pocket Problem V9/10 ****
A lot of good climbers threw themselves at this painfully obvious line until it was finally climbed by Brian Capps. Straight up the very overhanging northeast face via the widely spaced pockets, starting with your right hand in a sinker three-finger hole.

8. Black Heart V9 **
Just right of Pocket Problem. This goes from the platform to big huecos, via a huge toss off insultingly small holds.

North Face

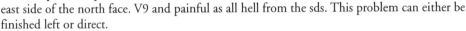

9. Terminate with Extreme Prejudice V8 **

Bust up and right from the hole on #8 to finish via the prominent black streak.

10. Ghost Dance V6 ****

This is the striking line on small pockets up the east side of the north face. V9 and painful as all hell from the sds. This problem can either be finished left or direct.

11. Moon Child V10 ***

This new line goes directly up from the mailbox-slot of #12. Make a move to a sloper pocket then trend up and left. Despo.

12. Old Bones V6 ***

Start low in the two-handed mailbox-slot right of the blank middle of the north face. Work right to a pocket, then cruise up past good holds to a right-hand bidoigt and left-hand pinch. Set up and huck for the distant lip. Nadir (V6), begins here and traverses all the way to the northwest prow and a finishing stance. Sequel (V2), starts here and busts right, traversing big holds to the hueco/ledge.

13. Second Coming V4 **

Start low in the pockets just right of #10 and fire for the big holes. Throw the exciting "Hail Mary" toss to the lip.

14. Lono V3 **

Start in the head-height, pancake-shaped hueco and go for a crimp. Same "Hail Mary" to finish.

15. Revolution V2 **

Take the hueco/ledge in the middle then top out straight up past less-than-obvious holds.

16. Revelation V1 *

Move right from the hueco/ledge to a mono, then up and over the northwest prow.

Mike Hickey, Millennium North Face
photo: Greg Johnson

THREE SISTERS

Krong playing on the Trailside Egg   photo: Adam Avery

THREE SISTERS PARK

Three Sisters Park is a mountainside of sporadic granite towers, miniature cliff bands and separate boulders that are easily reached from the myriad trail systems. This Jefferson County Open Space Park is a mixmaster of trails shared by hikers, bikers, runners, elk and deer. The boulders vary from very rough rock—rather taxing on the tips—to pain-free crimping; the top-outs on most blocks require dealing with lichen and grit. Losing interest? In the park's favor are some nice easy problems and a quiet setting with incredible views of Mt. Evans and Mt. Bierstadt.

Directions: Take Highway 74 from Morrison to Evergreen. From Evergreen take Highway 73 headed south (you can only go one way). Go 0.6 mile to the second stoplight and go right on Buffalo Park Road. Continue on this road past the high school for 1.5 miles to the parking area on the right.

***Make sure to pick up a trail map at the parking areas; there are about a million different trails around here.

Brothers Area: Walk up The Sisters Trail to a left on Ponderosa Trail. Pass The Brother's Lookout on the right and take a right on The Sisters Trail. Fifty yards down the trail, look up to the right into the woods, where Brothers Boulder can be seen.

South Face of The Brothers: The south face has a number of problems skirting the base. These problems are easy to locate as they are seen from Ponderosa Trail. A few uncharted blocks sit on the south hillside between The Brother and Ponderosa Trail.

Brothers Boulders

This is a pair of boulders sitting side by side approximately 75 yards east from The Sisters Trail. The left boulder is short and the right block stands a little over ten feet high.

Left Block

1. V1
A one-move problem on the left side.

2. V0
Straight up the face off the jug.

3. V5
A sds on the right side of the boulder starting off a full-pad edge then a terrible edge to the finish.

Right Block

1. V2 *
A traverse across the face through a sloping section.

2. V2 *
The left problem on decent edges to a dirty top-out.

3. V0
On the right side of the face above a small block is a decent warm-up.

The Sisters Area

The easiest way to reach these boulders is to walk Hidden Fawn Trail for 10 minutes to The Eggs. For Elephant Butt take the Hidden Fawn to the intersection with The Sisters Trail (15 minutes). To reach Energy Crag continue past the intersection for 45 yards and head up the hill to the west to reach both Energy Crag (100 yards) and The Blockheads (175 yards).

The Blockheads

This selection of boulders is located at the terminus of South Sister. The Sisters' ridgeline peters out before the north side of the Brothers. The main Blockhead is on the south end of South Sister. Numerous alluring west-facing slabs can be done along the ridge headed back north toward Middle Sister. Another way to find the Blockheads is to skirt the hillside headed east from Brothers Boulder past an old road/trail to the ridge between the Sisters and Brothers then head north about 40 yards towards the Sisters.

BLOCKHEAD

1. V2
The west face, up a discontinuous seam and edges.

2. V2
Up the white streak on the left above the block lying on the ground.

3. V3
Climb the right-facing corner off a white starting hold through the biggest part of the low roof.

4. V0 (not pictured)
The east-face gully, with a beautiful offset crack.

ENERGY CRAG

A condensed set of south-facing cracks and face problems on a short cliff band below The Blockheads (75 yards east). From The Sisters Trail/Hollow Fawn Trail intersection head south (45 yards) and the cliff band is above (100 yards west) from the Sisters Trail; it is located on the south side of a large northeast-facing slab. The problems listed are the main attractions with many more contrived problems offered.

Energy Crag; #4

1. Thievery V6 ***
On the left side of the crag is a burnt-orange face. Start low on the incut jug and move up the overhanging face to a full-pad edge then a left-hand sidepull to jugs. A great problem.

2. V3 *
Just right of Thievery is an arete. Climb up the laybacks and gastons using the feet on the adjacent wall.

3. V4 *
To the right of the dead tree is a low start off of an undercling to a right-hand slot then a tough mantle over the lip.

4. V4
Just right is a dynamic problem off an arete to a sloping top.

5. V0
The rightmost problem on the crag, with a small tree to climb through.

ELEPHANT BUTT

A squat little affair found at the junction of The Sisters Trail and Hidden Fawn Trail. The block is located 25 yards up The Sisters Trail on the right. There are some problems on this boulder, but they are extremely sharp and grating, and not worthy of a photo.

THE EGGS

These blocks—the best and most traveled—are easy to find as they are nestled directly off the Hidden Fawn Trail to the east less than a 10-minute walk from the parking area. A good landmark is a pair of signs indicating Area Closed Re-vegetation in Progress on the right 50 yards before passing the first Egg. A handful of additional small boulders with undocumented problems litter the hillside.

TRAILSIDE EGG

A chalk-infested block sitting 20 yards off the trail with problems on the south face. It is located just up Hidden Fawn Trail from tight turns in the trail and after the Area Closed signs. Many contrived problems can be done to lengthen a session on this block.

1. V0
The leftmost problem from a sds.

2. V1 **
The dihedral problem, with stemming, to gain a jug above.

3. V4 **
Just right of #2, on gold rock, is a tough little number. Start off a left-hand undercling and right-hand sidepull to gain a bad hold in the roof, then jugs.

4. V3 **
Climb the black rock on edges to high jugs. A sds is much harder.

5. V0 *
Follow a white streak right of the black patina face.

WEST CRACK EGG

This boulder is located approximately 30 yards up the hill to the east from Trailside Egg. It has a distinctive crack splitting its west side and a glued edge on the south face. No grades are given for the glued problems.

1. V2
The crack on the west face. The lower one starts, the harder it is.

In Between Egg

This is a few yards southeast from the West Crack Egg.

1. V3 **
A right-trending layback/crack starting on the west face. Dirty top-out. Moving left from the low starting holds is harder.

2. V1 *
A sds on the south face, off of decent sloping edges, to very good holds. Dirty top-out.

White Egg

South 20 feet from In Between Egg.

1. V1 *
On the north face, start off the jug and use an undercling to reach the top holds.

2. V2 *
Start on the white face then traverse to the left to jugs then the undercling to finish the problem.

Upper Egg

The best looking block on the hillside. It has a dihedral/scoop on the south side.

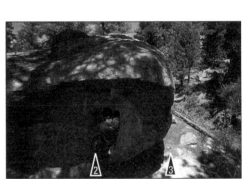

1. V0
The slab on the southwest face just left of the pine that hugs the boulder.

2. V6 **
Climb the dihedral/scoop. This is the best looking problem at the Eggs but it has the most vicious top-out so two stars will suffice. Climber at right is on this problem.

3. V4 *
The arete right of the dihedral, starting off the good jug. The roll onto the slab is not trivial. A direct start can be done off the horrible slopers just left of the starting hold.

4. V0 *
Climb the slab on the east face trying to find the hidden edges.

CASTLEWOOD CANYON

Mike Freischlag on the undone Red Slab, Inner Canyon   photo: Ken Kenney

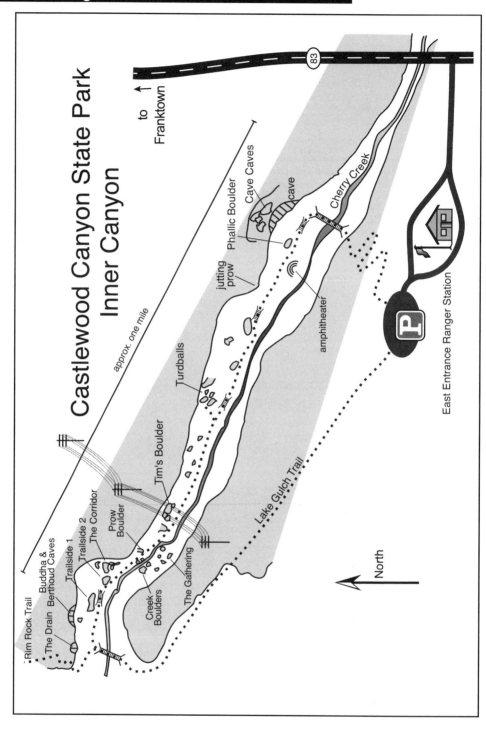

Castlewood Canyon State Park
Inner Canyon

to Franktown

83

approx. one mile

Cave Caves

Phallic Boulder

cave

Cherry Creek

jutting prow

amphitheater

Turdballs

Tim's Boulder

Lake Gulch Trail

The Corridor

Trailside 2

Trailside 1

Prow Boulder

Buddha & Berthoud Caves

The Drain

Rim Rock Trail

Creek Boulders

The Gathering

North

East Entrance Ranger Station

P

CASTLEWOOD CANYON

Some love it, some hate it, but thankfully, most avoid it. Perhaps it's the fact that almost all the good areas are hidden behind thick copses of unforgiving scrub oak, or perhaps it's the rock quality, which can vary from perfect to downright horrible, even on established problems. In any case, Castlewood Canyon has revealed itself through ongoing development to be a complex and multi-faceted area with enough potential to entertain creative boulderers for years to come.

Recent activity has focused on the Inner Canyon, a sunny, pleasant canyon to the south and east of Castlewood proper. The south-facing walls on the canyon's north side provide a maze of sunny blocks and sheltered caves that are climbable through the winter, making the Inner Canyon viable even after monster dumps. A handful of good boulders have been developed in the forested shady side, though the rock can be mossy. For boulderers who can appreciate the aesthetics of an area, not just the bouldering, Castlewood is hard to beat. Spend an afternoon playing on the tucked-away boulders above the quiet trickle of Cherry Creek and see if you don't get hooked!

Inner Canyon
Directions: From I-25 take exit 182 at Castle Rock. Follow Wilcox Street to Fifth Street and turn left, heading east on State Route 86 to Franktown. Once in Franktown turn south on State Route 83, which you follow 4.7 miles to a sign for Castlewood Canyon State Park. Turn right, drive a half-mile to the entrance station and (unless you have an annual State Parks Pass) pay a $5 entrance fee. Follow the road to the Canyon Point Parking Area (the westernmost lot).

Follow the Inner Canyon Trail north out of the parking lot and down into the Canyon (five minutes). Cross the bridge over Cherry Creek and you're there. The bouldering areas are arrayed along the canyon walls heading east/west from this point. With a little exploration, you'll find a myriad of bouldering possibilities not described herein on the vertical mini-cliffs that line the base of the canyon's north side, with the vast majority of the problems in the V0-V3 range.

In addition to the areas described in the text, here are three interesting areas, for which we've provided minimal beta. Explore and enjoy.

The Swamp
This excellent area is 200 yards east of the bridge where the Inner Canyon Trail first crosses the creek. Locate a cigar-shaped rock leaning against a lower tier of the south-facing north rim. A west-facing wall right at the cigar lies above an often wet area that affords a great traverse. The whole area has dozens of problems in the V0-V7 range.

Cobble in a Blender
This short but sweet wall is just off the trail on the shady south rim of the canyon. Just as the trail breaches the rim, bushwhack left (west) about 80 feet to a notch/bowl in the rim. The wall is down and west, just past the jumble of dead trees and boulders. A handful of decent up-problems have been done but the main attraction is the traverse, a strenuous left-to-right affair on jutting crystals that finishes by climbing up the rightmost problem by the tree.

The Cave Caves
On a stealthy bench above Castlewood's largest cave, these funky blocks offer roof problems in a Hueco Tanks-like setting. Cross the bridge, hike directly uphill (north), skirt east around the huge cave, and scramble to the upper bench (4th class). Don't miss Jonah and the Whale (V5), a unique traverse in the deepest floor of these chambers. It starts low and right on a SW-facing section. Move left on the low rail to its end; follow the upper rail back up and punch straight up above the start.

TIM'S BOULDER (POWERLINES)

This excellent, overhanging wall sits directly below the high-tension power lines that cross the canyon, offering some of the smoothest and steepest rock at Castlewood.

Tim's Boulder

Directions: Head up the hill from the trail once you reach the power lines. The boulder is just below the cliff line in a cluster of blocks. It is a very overhanging, southwest-facing white wall

1. Tiger Woods V7 ***

The leftmost line out the cave. Start on double underclings and bust past the huge, sloping hole to a good flake, then the chossy lip.

2. Pain V5 *

From a painful, incut undercling hole, six feet right of #1, move up to a bad sloper in the horizontal crack then throw for a bucket.

3. Flakes of Wrath V3 **

Begin on #2 but move right into a good pocket then follow the flake system diagonally up and left to finish. Thuggy.

THE CORRIDOR AREA

This curiously neglected zone didn't see much action until the late 90s, despite its obvious array of large, clean blocks perched above a scenic bend in the canyon. The Corridor itself provides superb V1-V3 vertical face climbs on smooth, tan-and-green stone with surprisingly difficult top-outs. The long, vertical wall one tier down from The Corridor offers a myriad of decent face problems in the V1-V4 range, while a taller set of walls on the benches to the south and east of The Corridor offers highball versions of the same.

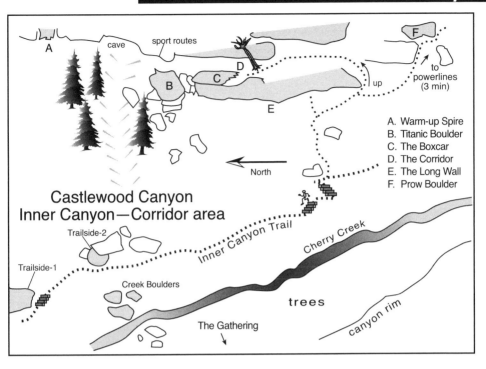

**Castlewood Canyon
Inner Canyon—Corridor area**

cave
sport routes
A
D
C
B
E
up
F
to powerlines (3 min)

North

A. Warm-up Spire
B. Titanic Boulder
C. The Boxcar
D. The Corridor
E. The Long Wall
F. Prow Boulder

Inner Canyon Trail
Cherry Creek
Trailside-2
Trailside-1
Creek Boulders
trees
canyon rim
The Gathering

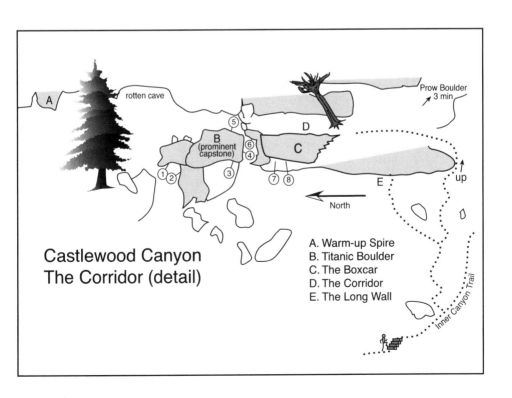

**Castlewood Canyon
The Corridor (detail)**

A
rotten cave
B (prominent capstone)
C
D
E
Prow Boulder 3 min
up
North
Inner Canyon Trail

A. Warm-up Spire
B. Titanic Boulder
C. The Boxcar
D. The Corridor
E. The Long Wall

Directions: After the power lines, just before the trail descends via stairs to the creek, cut up and right around a boulder and head directly uphill to Long Wall. Head right (south) around Long Wall then back north to reach the upper bench where The Corridor sits.

A. Warm-up Spire

Just left of a rotten cave, 50 feet up the hill from the enormous ponderosa pine is this tall, slabby, spire-like feature on the canyon rim. Though the problems aren't exceptionally hard (V0-V2), they do provide good warm-ups on nice stone. The aesthetic black wall to the right has toprope bolts on top but can be bouldered out, sort of.

B. The Titanic

Easily visible from the canyon floor, this enormous block can be recognized by its black, overhanging west face high up in a jumble of rocks. Many steep, hard problems are found in the network of caves under and around this block.

1. Soice in a Blender V7 **

This long problem is in a grotto/pit just below and north of The Titanic. Start with your right hand in a mouth-pocket up and left around the corner in the cave. Drop down on cobbles, trend right around the corner, then punch straight up the white face. V2 from the stand-up.

2. Kate Winslet V5 **

Chubby yet appealing! This technical problem climbs the scooped face on the south side of the grotto. Start on rough slopers and traverse right to the arete, then out the arete on cobbles. V7 and crimpy if you start all the way right.

3. King of the World V6 ***

The only problem done so far on the prominent west face. Sds in the horizontal crack and head for the obvious hueco. Spectacular position.

4. Pit Monkey V6 **

Start on a good hueco in the pit below #3. Move right to the arete, traverse around the corner on pockets, and finish out on the orange face over the bad landing.

5. Grease Monkey V9 **

Powerful stuff. Sds at the base of a triangular, four-foot long depression in the east cave. Bust into bad underclings and power up.

6. Ass Monkey V3 **

Just across the cave from the finish of #4. Start on the jug horn, head left to the arete and make a long pull to the lip.

C. THE BOXCAR

With a proud one-bolt sport lead on its north face, this cherry block forms the western wall of the Corridor.

7. Scott's Wall V3 ** 🪨

Five feet to the left, just before the landing craps out. Climb the faint black streak on small crimps, heading for a juggy bowl near the lip of the boulder. Airy!

8. Scott's Folly V1 🪨

On the west face over the big bench, just left of the wall's center. Climb friable incuts up the vertical wall in the wide black streak. A couple of good highballs at V0+ can be done further right.

D. THE CORRIDOR

This sunny zone offers countless good up-problems in the V1-V3 range along its 50-foot length, as well as a crimpy right-to-left V4 traverse on the east wall. The walls to the south offer good, high warm-ups over pine needle landings.

The Corridor

E. THE LONG WALL

One tier down from the Corridor, this is the first wall you hit on the way up the hill. It has numerous V1-V4 problems on crimpers and cobbles up dark, varnished stone. The very leftmost line is a good V2 highball, while Pebbly Blue Dot (V5) takes a line between two trees right of center.

F. THE PROW BOULDER

Descend southeast from The Corridor, passing below the Juggernaut Boulders (two huge chunks of worthless conglomerate on the cliff line). Fifty feet southeast of these you will find this obvious southwest-facing wall with a prominent, white prow on the right.

1. Proud Pile V2 *

Climb the corner sprinkled with rock lettuce via a good crack on the right wall.

2. Pile Proud V4 ** 🪨

Start three feet right of the corner with your left hand on a pocket/pinch, swing right to a good cobble then over the roof. Strenuous and committing.

3. Kind Hole V1 *** 🪨

A classic jug haul. Tweak the yellow quartz knob to hit the perfect hueco, then head over the bulge on jugs.

4. The Shaft Arete (aka SMC) V5 *** 🕐 🔦

The painfully obvious double arete up the south-facing nose of the block. Horrendous landing, which can be ameliorated somewhat by the clever use of pad technology.

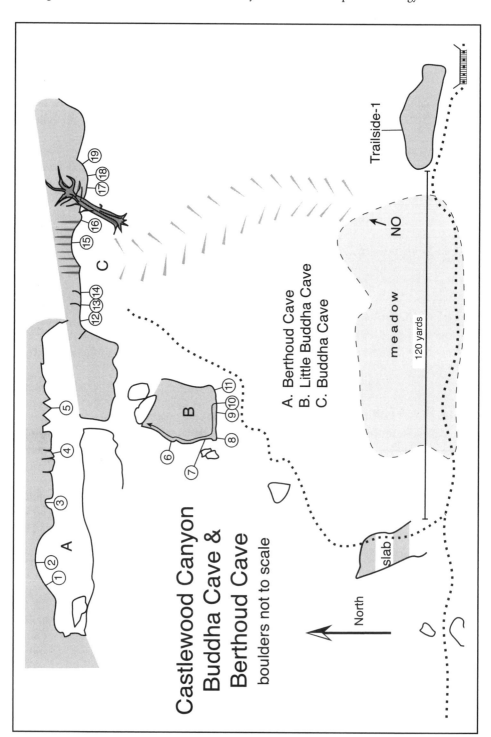

Castlewood Canyon
Buddha Cave &
Berthoud Cave
boulders not to scale

A. Berthoud Cave
B. Little Buddha Cave
C. Buddha Cave

Trailside-1

meadow

120 yards

NO

North

slab

THE BUDDHA AND BERTHOUD CAVES

Though a bit of a trudge (20 minutes), these caves offer Castlewood's highest concentration of steep problems in a stealthy hang well out of sight of the trail. This is not a very good place to warm up. The roofy nature and southern exposure of these walls guarantees their climbability even in the worst of conditions, though the top may drip with run-off.

Directions: 120 yards down from Trailside Boulder One (an enormous block on the trail just above a red footbridge and just downcanyon from the stairs), after the meadow, you'll see a slab on the right. Climb along this slab, head uphill another 50 feet then diagonal right towards the caves through scrub oak.

A. THE BERTHOUD CAVE

Named after one of Colorado's finer hamlets, this grainy yet sunny attraction offers one of the largest horizontal roofs in the Front Range (and a bellyful of bad puns). Come early in the day with fresh skin and some snap in your arms, otherwise you'll hate the place. Although the problems can be finished at the lip of the cave (subtract a V-grade), real climbers will ante up for the headwall above.

1. After Berthoud V6 *

Match hands in a perfectly round three-foot diameter hueco in the left side of the cave, sitting down with your head pointed east. Work past underclings and knee bars into the huge bowl. Climb out the left side of the bowl to a big cobble at the lip, then head straight over the tan-colored bulge to a highball finish. Off-routing the jugs in the back of the bowl and crossing the bowl through its middle to join the sloping rail on the cave finish of #2 is V8 ***.

2. Giving Berthoud V8 **

Start 20 feet back in the cave, with your hands on the lip of a huge (body-sized) hole, and your head oriented south. Punch out to the huge bowl, then make a big move out with your right

hand to a sloping, crystalline rail. Work right on the rail to the lip, then realm up the black streak past "the football" to finish. Finishing straight out the bowl into #1 is The Placenta, V5.

3. Berthoud Canal V5 *

Ohh, is it ever! This dynamic line out the obvious scoop on the right side of the cave offers fun, contorted moves on solid holds. Sds low at the bottom of the scoop, then out past holes to the lip. Reel left over the lip to top out, then jump to the pads. A super-low, butt-dragging start seems quite hard.

4. Berthoud Hips V7 **

Just right of the cave proper is a small brown buttress with a flared, black crack on its left side. Sds by underclinging an enormous, oblong bowl. Crank up, then move right onto crystals embedded in the buttress to finish. Sustained and powerful.

5. J.T's Prow V4

This is the middle one of three aretes/fins to the right of the cave. Fall off high and you might find yourself 20 feet lower, back down at the Buddha Cave.

B. LITTLE BUDDHA BOULDER

Not so little at all, this attractive cube with a very overhanging south face sits just 40 feet downhill and southwest of the Buddha Cave. Like all the best stuff at Castlewood, the rock on the south wall is blessed with an iron-hard white veneer, the result of calcification. The plumb line up the middle of the face has yielded a very difficult boulder problem.

6. West Face V1-V2

A host of short but interesting problems up pebbles and pockets on the solid west face.

7. Deuto's Face V2 *

Start four feet left of the southwest arete with your left hand on top of a huge embedded plaque/cobble, stretch high and right for a jug pocket, then up the face.

8. Monkey Shots V7 **

The southwest corner of the block, working holds on both sides of the arete to a grueling top-out.

9. The Crystal Method V9 ****

The very steep central line up the wall, moving right from the sharp, jutting cobble to a sinker three-finger pocket in the white streak.

10. J.T.'s Arete V4 *

This line would be perfect if not for the grainy bulge top-out. With your right hand in a good hole around the southeast arete, bust up to a licheny horizontal then master the terrifying bulge maneuver.

11. Deuto's Traverse V5 **

This 35-foot long gem is a blast! Start on the rightmost pocket on the south face, move left around the arete on good holes, punch up to the good right-hand pocket on #2 and head left again to the northwest arete (V0).

C. THE BUDDHA CAVE

Endowed with flat, piney landings and a warm southern exposure, this mini-amphitheater of good, solid rock also offers a short ice pillar in colder weather. The problems are generally powerful with long moves to good cobbles and crimpers. Finish the majority of the problems by dropping back to the pads from the dirt-covered ledge.

12. The Buddha V4 ***
Sds on an oval-shaped hueco under the prow then bust past good holds into the overhanging corner. Beware the loose flake high and right!

13. Ned's Corner V5 *
Sds six feet right over a flat block, your hands low in a hole. Hit cobbles over the lip then crimp your way up the vertical corner above. Devious.

14. Rounded Prow V3 *
Start with your right hand in a good, waist-high three-finger pocket then amble up the rounded buttress on slopers and pebbles. Descend the dirty V0 corner just right.

15. Sometimes Wet V2 **
Just under the right side of the drainage, this little unit climbs the black streak from its lowest point on the wall. Sds and crank past good holes, then drop from the sandy lip.

16. Phillip's Problem V5 ***
Just what is his problem anyway? Sds directly under the rightmost portion of the streak in the bowl/cave, then make a big move to a flat incut cobble. V5+ if you reel right and top out on #17.

17. Butt Crystal V3 *
Start low in a good two-hand "mouth," hit a horn and go left to a cobble then up. Bizarre and trickier than it looks.

18. Swirly Face V3 *
Start on the guano-stained pillar/heap, shoulder roll to a super-incut pocket, then pimp up the swirls above.

19. Slime Pile V1
The rightmost problem on the wall climbs past holes to a choss-filth top-out. Horrible.

THE DRAIN

This cobble-studded attraction has the added benefit of being completely protected from the elements by an enormous roof overhead. As the remotest area in the Inner Canyon, this is a good place to start the day if you intend to work eastward. The overhanging, juggy nature of the rock makes this an ideal place to warm up, with many variations possible.

Directions: Continue west on the trail, passing a "Leaves of three, let it be" sign. Just before the trail dips down to a bridge at Cherry Creek, turn right and follow a faint trail uphill to the cliff line. The Drain sits below a large roof, recognizable from the canyon floor.

1. You Pay, Hot Tea V4 **
Right over the bad, rocky landing. Start on #2 but shoulder roll right hand to a pinch then work your way out the cave above. Add a V-grade if you traverse in from the horizontal crack in the sandy cave 30 feet right.

2. The Drain V2 **
Directly above the leftmost portion of the good landing. Sds matched in a hole and work past jugs and pebbles to a sloping dish finish. Add a V-grade if you traverse in.

3. The Full Drain V7 ***
The 70+ foot-long integral traverse of the wall. Begin on the wall's very right margin where it's a whopping four-feet tall. Battle along the pebble-studded lip for 20+ feet until you join the main traverse. Move into #1, hit the lip and continue left along a giant, square hueco, stepping off when the wall turns slabby.

ELEVENMILE CANYON

Krong on the Roadside Boulder   photo: Droeger

ELEVENMILE CANYON STATE PARK

This park is vast, beautiful, and has many inspiring views of the Sangre de Cristo and Collegiate Peaks. Cliff bands on the reservoir's north side host many boulderfields, scattered through the aspen groves at a safe distance from the weekend hordes. There are a healthy serving of new problems in a quiet environment, as long as you venture off into the woods. If there is much wind, it'll be howling over the reservoir, but the weather is usually just as pleasant as the scenery.

Sadly, on the beaten track, the park is a mess. Campgrounds abound like flies on manure, and inconsiderate fishermen, indigenous rednecks and white trash leave beer cans along the water's edge without a thought.

Directions: From Lake George on US Route 24 head west out of town. Turn left at 0.7 mile on Park County Road 92 (Eleven Mile/Spring Mountain State Park). Drive 9.8 miles to the Ranger Station and continue past (on the left of the Ranger Station) to Park County Road 335.

Grove Boulders: Go right on CR335 and drive 1.0 mile (just past a wire fence) and take a right on a dirt road. Continue on this road 0.8 mile over a small knoll (rocky section) and stay headed west along a fence-line to the set of boulders, which are roadside.

Lauf Boulders: Stay on CR335 for 2.4 miles after the turn off CR92. The boulders (visible from the road) are on the north side of CR335 before entering the Tiara Subdivision.

GROVE BOULDERS

These four boulders are situated in an idyllic setting; aspens shade the problems and the seclusion from the park's many visitors is a welcome relief.

FENCE BOULDER

The block closest to the fence-line, and the first encountered from the road.

1. V0 *
The problem right of the south face downclimb. One move from the low slopers to a big jug rail.

2. V1
Climb the left seam on the east face.

3. V2 *
Climb the middle seam on the east face.

4. V1
Climb the right, wide, seam on the east face. A tad dirty. Alright, filthy.

5. V0 (not pictured)
On the north face climb the right side slab.

6. V0 *
Climb the west face left-facing dihedral.

GROVE BOULDER

This block, with a crystal-covered east face, is 20 yards west of Fence Boulder. Bring some extra flesh.

1. V1 * (not pictured)
Climb the right side of the south face.

2. Map of England V3 *
Climb the left side of the east face on sharp edges.

3. V4
Climb straight up the east face on micro edges. Very sharp!

4. V2
A painful dynamic problem on the right side of the east face.

PERFECT SLAB

A beautiful boulder 20 yards west of the Grove Boulder.

1. V1 *
The left arete on the west face. Jump start to a good right-hand edge then up the arete.

2. V3 *
Climb the left side of the west face on bomber, albeit tiny, edges. A good problem!

3. V3 *
Climb the middle of the west face off a low layback. Hard to get situated on the face.

LAUF BOULDERS

These very fine to decent blocks are situated on the north side of CR335 with a spectacular view to the southwest. Other boulders with good potential are to the east under the cliff.

ROADSIDE BOULDER

This awesome boulder is clearly visible from the road and only a 50 yard stroll.

1. V2
Climb up the flake on the right side of the west face.

2. V0
The downclimb on the southwest arete.

3. V1 *
Climb the slightly overhanging edges left of the aspen on the east face.

4. V2
Climb the thin slab right of the aspen on the east face.

5. White Caps V5 **
The superb northeast arete starting low and finishing on the east face.

6. V2 **
Right of #5 climb the small dihedral with a hard start.

LAST LAUF

Straight up the hill approximately 70 yards from Roadside Boulder is this pointy boulder.

1. V2 *

This problem is on the west side.

LAUF BLOCK

This tall boulder, with a small overhanging block on its west side, is located 50 yards due east from the Roadside Boulder in the aspens.

1. V0

Climb the west face off a huge incut jug system.

2. V4

Climb the fragile and thin left side of the south face.

3. V2

Climb the southeast arete and finish on the south face.

4. V0

Climb up the east face on good holds.

LITTLE LAUF

The overhanging block attached to the west face of the Lauf Block.

1. Ich bin Einfach Gut V5

A sds on the left side of the overhang. A rather painful encounter with the rock face.

2. V0

Climb the right-facing corner right of #1.

Central
Mountains

GETTING AROUND THE CENTRAL MOUNTAINS

Colorado's Central Mountains, with their abundance of ski areas, is a growing recreation center. If you are unfamiliar with the region a detailed map is recommended for travel to the various climbing areas. As mentioned elsewhere, this guidebook assumes a basic knowledge of the state and/or the resources to find small cities. The map below is provided for those who have forgotten their state map at home or are suffering from momentary geographic amnesia. It is assumed that the author's written descriptions in conjunction with this map will be adequate to locate the specific climbing areas.

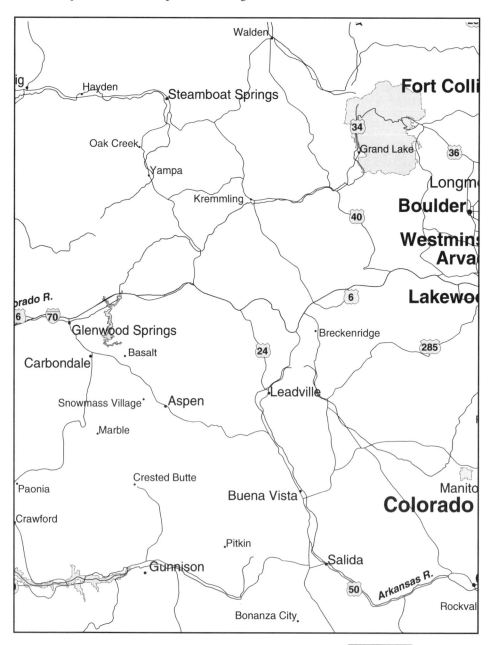

STEAMBOAT SPRINGS

Danger Rockwell at Fish Creek Falls   photo: Krong

STEAMBOAT SPRINGS

The bouldering in and around Steamboat may have nothing on the excellent skiing, mountain biking and rafting, but what bouldering exists is pretty good. If you need a fix, and your fingers are not soft mush from sitting in the hot springs, two areas can be reached very easily within 10 minutes from the town's main drag.

FISH CREEK FALLS

The definition of a quick-fix bouldering session. Problems range from V0 to V?. The base of the crag offers a few fun problems and a couple of boulders near the cliff can be exploited for a decent pump. The views from this boulderfield are incredible!

Directions: From Lincoln Avenue turn right on 3rd Street then right on Fish Creek Falls Road. Drive 2.9 miles to the parking area on the left. Additional parking is just up the road a short distance. From the first parking area walk up the paved sidewalk next to the road (towards the other parking area). Take the rocky path on the left (heading north) and walk for a few minutes staying on the main trail. The trail hits the obvious crag and surrounding mini-blocks. The crag has a few bolted lines and a great view of Fish Creek Falls.

WEST RABBIT EARS PASS

A quiet boulderfield just off the turmoil of US40. A few years ago a handful of problems were developed, but neglect over the past couple of years have left them devoid of chalk and flesh. A motivated climber could easily get a substantial pump and possible first ascents. The completed problems are hard to discern as spider webs and lichen has taken a hold once again. Problems range from V0 short slabs to V8.

Directions: From Steamboat drive up US40 towards Rabbit Ears Pass 7.8 miles from the junction of Highway 131 and US 40. A long pullout is on the right with a sign indicating a $1370 fine for shooting moose. The pullout is between mile markers 144 and 145. From Rabbit Ears Pass summit the pullout is 9.8 miles. From the middle of the pullout walk down the hillside 75 yards on a faint trail past a large cliff to the boulders.

SOUTHWEST RABBIT EAR BOULDER

The main block, down the hillside from the cliffs nearest the highway. The boulder is discernible by a large flat top that is easy to gain with a mere hop. A small cave is on the northeast side. Some wooden pallets are strewn below the boulder to add a white-trash feel to the area.

1. Show Me V5 **

The problem starting inside the small cave on the left side. The small block to the left is off.

2. Weather Report V5 *

On the left side of the taller east face. Start low below the small block then move up and right to the top. A V6 traverses in from the left and finishes on Weather Report.

3. Munjal Traverse V4 *

Start low on the south face (left of #2) and traverse up and left on good holds to finish on a scary top-out.

4. V0

To the left of #3 is a straight-up problem on the far left face.

Down the hillside to the south is a reported V8 called Six Shooter. Tons more bouldering is within spitting distance.

Dave Whaley on Arch Enemy Slab   photo: Phillip Benningfield

SOUTH PLATTE

The immensity of the Platte region provides a near-endless supply of bouldering possibilities, although many of the boulders, on closer inspection, are nothing short of piles. A handful of areas, namely Turkey Rock, Sheep's Nose, Sphinx Rock and Glen Elk have easy access and occasionally really prime granite—never underestimate the new problems to be found—nor, for that matter, old forgotten gems from the days of yesteryear.

Directions:

Sphinx Rock
From Denver: Take US Route 285 past Conifer to Pine Junction. Go left (headed south) on Road 126 (Pine Valley Road) for 6.5 miles to Pine. Turn left on Jefferson County Road 83. Drive 0.4 mile to parking on the left or right of road. Sphinx Rock (the cliff band on the right that houses the famous overhanging splitter Sphinx Crack) is a two-minute hike to the east and easy to see.

From South Colorado: Take State Route 67 from Woodland Park to Deckers then continue north on Jefferson County Road 126 to Pine and follow directions above.

Glen Elk Boulder
From Pine, drive east on Jefferson County Road 83 (past the ever-popular Bucksnort Inn) to a lone boulder next to the road (with an adjacent one-car pullout) before entering the small enclave of Glen Elk. The block sits next to Elk Creek. From US Route 285 at Conifer, you can also continue west to a left on South Elk Creek Road, drive south through Glen Elk and just after passing through the town the block is on your right, by the creek and visible from the road

Sheep's Nose
From State Route 67 (Douglas County 73) turn in Westcreek and drive 0.2 miles to a stop sign and left turn on Westcreek Road. Drive 0.6 miles to Stump Road (Douglas County 68) and turn right and drive 1.8 miles to a dirt pullout on the right. Walk north past a fence on a washed-out road approximately 150 yards to a cairn. Take the trail leading right uphill approximately 175 yards to a boulder with a horizontal crack filled with crystals (The Dinosaur Boulder). The boulders begin uphill towards Sheep's Nose.

Turkey Rock
Follow Sheep's Nose directions and continue on Stump Road to FR 360 (a sign for Big Turkey Campground and Turkey Rock). Take a right and drive to the campground (the road can be a tad treacherous for 2x2 cars). Park at the campground and follow directions given with each area.

GLEN ELK BOULDER

A lone block with a handful of fun problems on solid, featured granite. This boulder sits in a meadow next to Elk Creek with old, tattered Private Property signs tacked to trees down the road. When visiting this block be discreet, and respect the landowner (if this is actually private land).

1. V1 *
The far left arete on the west face.

2. V0
Climb up the dirty, low-angle dihedral with the terrible landing.

3. V6 **
A low start right of the dihedral with a difficult reach from the starting holds. Easier from a high start off of #2.

4. The Cheater V4 **
A super cheater stone start up the middle of the west face. A low start would be extremely difficult.

5. V3 **
Climb the overhanging right flake of the west face finishing the same as #4. Flop finish—probably the crux.

6. V0
Climb the south-face seam.

7. V1
Just right of #6 on the south face, up discontinuous seams.

SPHINX PARK BOULDERS

The huge split blocks under the ultra-classic Sphinx Crack. If you get off on wildly committing barn-door laybacks, you'll love this place. There are more stout-looking aretes in this boulderfield than just about anywhere. If you are inclined to venture up the bigger ones, bring as many pads and spotters as you can muster up. The problems included here are just the tip of the iceberg.

SPLIT BOULDERS

Two of the main chiseled boulders down and left from Sphinx Crack. The boulders are white, with a distinct crack splitting them in half.

1. V0 **

The crack in the middle of the blocks. A desperate slab is to the right and sickeningly high arete to the left.

2. V2

The arete right of the crack behind the tree. Climbing the arete from the opposite side is V3.

THE SLAB

There are too many big, ugly slabs to give each one a slabular name. This block sits in the lowest boulderfield under Sphinx Crack, closer to the creek, and just outside the largest blocks with chasms leading through them. A haphazard firepit sits next to the face.

V3 *

The thin fragile slab, facing south, that exits to the right.

SHEEP'S NOSE BOULDERS

The blocks under Sheep's Nose vary from crystal-infested horrorfests to perfect granite with incut edges and nice landings (see Air Jordan). The boulders included here are all found most easily after locating the best block, which is the Air Jordan Boulder (included for its superb quality and as a useful landmark). Many of the taller faces in the near vicinity have toprope anchors from old bouldering/toprope competitions; with the advent of pads most of these taller faces can be done in relative safety. Ha-ha-ha!

AIR JORDAN BOULDER

All boulders, whether granite or sandstone or limestone, should have the qualities of Air Jordan! The boulder is just the right height at 15-odd feet, square for the most part, solid but for the intermittent chip or flake, with one line for downclimbing, and great landings (although extra pads help out on one or two problems). It is hard to think of anything which would improve the Air Jordan experience; possibly one more tree for shade—but the tree would be detrimental to worthy photos. The boulder shows its undying popularity by the number of nubbins, all over the rock, caked in chalk, even on desperate topropes, or possible new problems (that were probably done by some tennis-shoe clad guy in painter pants back when I was a wee lad). And lastly the boulder has a sumptuous view of Pikes Peak to add flavor to the already tasty scenery.

Directions: From The Dinosaur Boulder you will pass numerous blocks covered in Colorado Bouldering. Continue past these boulders staying on the trails that head northwest around the talus slopes. Walk past the obvious chalked boulders staying below most of the blocks to the northwest. After passing a firepit (if you happen to run into it) continue to the northwest for 90 yards to a big west-facing boulder that looks better than any of the others on the hillside. The boulder lies on the western edge of the huge boulderfield leading down from Sheep's Nose.

1. V0 (not pictured)
The left side of the north face, up diagonal jugs. Also the downclimb. There are a couple of desperate looking lines to the left through the steep east face: done, undone?

2. V2 ** (not pictured)
The sloping face before the right arete of the north face.

3. V3 * (not pictured)
Climb the northwest arete from a low start.

4. The Waffler V3 *
This might be a new one—but it might not! Climb the northwest face starting from #5 then moving directly left to a hidden edge and the top.

5. V4 ****
This problem is on the cusp of classic, it received three stars in the first guide, so what the hell—it gets four here! Climb the left side of the west face off good sidepulls to a big reach up high and right.

6. V5 ***
Can't quite muster the vote for four stars. The rock is bing-bing but the moves are a tad unrelenting. Climb straight up the edges and undercling to the flat jugs in the middle of the west face.

7. V3 ****
This one gets all the stars! It looks like a great granite line and climbs like one as well. The problem ventures up the right arete of the west face with an interesting top-out (i.e. CRUX).

8. V?
An unknown line leading off of #7 that looks and feels difficult. A perfect flat landing for the mandatory leap to the 18-foot high lip.

9. V?
This one has a hazard factor. One just can't tell if a bad fall will send you into the adjacent block. There are definitely big reaches up high after pinner micro-edges to begin the festivities. I think I once heard—this may be the definition of sandbag—that the problem was 5.12+. The first moves feel that hard and left my flesh in disarray. A bolt is on top.

AIR JORDAN SATELLITES

VOs Slab

V2

VOS SLAB

A long slab with numerous dirty V0s through the horizontal breaks. The block is a mere 15 yards southeast from His Airness.

V4

V2 *

A golden overhang due east from AJ 20 yards. Walk under a giant fallen tree and past V0s Slab to get there.

V4 *

A double arete problem that is a tad dirty, due north from AJ. Bring pads.

Golden Dihedral V4 **

Uphill from Air Jordan to the northeast approximately 80 yards on a very faint trail. The boulder is actually visible from Air Jordan, if you have a keen eye for chalk and bolts; a large tree sits in front of the dihedral. The problem begins low on well-chalked edges and leads out right in a seam to a right-facing dihedral. Bolts on top.

ADDITIONAL BLOCKS

These are found uphill from Air Jordan and below Ten Years After (the huge right-facing dihedral on Sheep's Nose)

V4 **

Uphill from Air Jordan to the northwest approximately 125 yards. This block is due west from Golden Dihedral with the bolts on top. The boulder is fin-shaped and it has an east-facing overhang with a couple of variations.

THE LARGE ONE BOULDER (NOT PICTURED)

This massive block (it appears to be the biggest on the hillside) sits 25 yards from Sheep's Nose, down and right from Ten Years After. There are three hard problems on the steep south face that stay shaded on hot days. A handful of other lines circumnavigate the boulder and its buddy blocks to offer a few desperate-looking lines on gorgeous lichen-striped faces.

WASH BOULDERS

These granite boulders are littered along the hillside below the west face of Sheep's Nose. The boulders here are not as cute as the Air Jordan boulders but a line or two show some cloning to be occurring. Feel free to keep an open mind and explore the area more thoroughly: boulders line the hillside like hippies at a Dead concert. To reach them walk along the hillside from Air Jordan staying at the same level, give or take a few feet, for 200 to 250 yards. The boulders appear as the woods open up into small meadows above the sandy wash.

WASHOUT BOULDER

The first real block that appears to have some bouldering opportunities. The boulder, with problems on the west face, sits 40 yards from the wash.

1. V0
The far left side of the southwest face.

2. Adventure Bouldering Part One V5
The hard south bulge problem on very questionable rock. Be careful laddy.

SECOND BOULDER

Couldn't come up with a better name at 11:50 p.m. This block is 45 yards north from The Washout.

1. V0 (not pictured)
Climb the easy right-trending ledge on the north face.

2. V2 *
Up the northwest face, near the aspen, from a low start.

3. V0
Climb the south face's right-trending ledge.

4. V0 (not pictured)
Climb the southeast bulge.

Mouth Boulder

This boulder with a horizontal seam along its lower expanse is located to the north 20 yards from Second Boulder.

V3

Climb the vertical seam on the west face. Much harder from a sds.

Tonsils Boulder

This block is directly behind the Mouth to the northeast.

1. V1

Climb the left arete on the southwest face and left of the good flake.

2. V0 *

Go from the flake to the horizontal and top out on the southwest face.

3. V0

Climb the short arete to the right of #2.

Fifth Boulder

I'm getting quite creative with the names. This mean boulder is 30 yards north of the Mouth.

Wash Your Mouth Out V4

This one doesn't get a star due to the pain factor. Start high and muckle through the sharp crystal and seam. A low start would be even more fun.

Smashing Boulder

This block has two very fun—one might even say smashing—problems on the northeast face, and a jump for a downclimb. The boulder has a number of other lines to be completed.

1. It's a Wash V1 *

Climb the beautiful vertical northeast face in the middle utilizing the sloping left arete.

2. V2 **

Climb the right side of the northeast face on very good holds.

Turkey Rock Area-South Side Boulders

A massive area filled to overflowing with hundreds of boulders; some chossy, some scrumptious. A few of the developed ones are listed below.

Directions: From Campsite #3 take the closed dirt road to the south and continue approximately 150 yards to the silver gate. The boulders are past the gate to the northwest.

1. Crack Boulder Problem V? ***

This boulder sits 75 yards past the silver gate and up the hillside to the west 60 yards. A classic line that couldn't be more obvious as one jams the off-hands right-leaning crack. This is more than likely a toprope as a fall from up high might shatter a femur.

2. V1

Obvious little cracked boulder 35 yards behind and to the west from Crack Boulder.

3. V2

Crumbly arete on the boulder adjacent to the V1 crack.

Little Aretes Area

These little blocks are small and safe: a nice respite from the highball affairs. The blocks can be located by continuing down the dirt road past the silver gate to a haggard old barbed-wire fence. Then walk west up the fence-line to the first Little Arete.

Fence Arete

Fence Arete V4 *

The arete problem next to the fence, with a weird start to a double arete.

Little Left Arete

This block is next door to the Little Right Arete and located 20 yards south from the Fence Arete; the boulder stretches a mere 10 feet tall.

1. V3

Climb the overhanging east face from a hard start to a mantle on the slab.

2. V0

The right-leaning arete on the northwest face.

V0s

LITTLE RIGHT ARETE

The boulder sitting next to Little Left Arete.

1. V0
A couple of easy lines on the south and west faces.

2. V0
The right side of the south face.

NORTH ARETE BLOCK

This singular boulder sits 30 yards to the north of the Little Aretes.

1. Running Fart V2 *
A ridiculous running start problem on the left side of the south face to bad little slopers and a flop finish.

2. Brain Fart V1
Only a fool would do this crumbling mass on the southwest arete.

TURKEY TAIL - NORTH SIDE BOULDERS

From campsite #8 walk up the only trail (10-15 minutes) headed to the north face of Turkey Tail and the gap to reach the south face of Turkey Perch.

ARCH ENEMY SLAB

A spectacular slab tooth sitting on the north face of Turkey Tail and next to the trail. Two boulders to the east offer more problems in the V-easy range.

1. V2 **
Climb up the huge northwest slab from the left to reach the high seam.

2. V1 **
The right arete on the northwest face to the high seam.

3. V0 ** (not pictured)
Climb the double arete on the south face—this is also the downclimb.

Turkey Perch Boulders

These boulders can be reached from the south side by walking through the jumbled masses below Rooster Tail and Turkey Tail and by some houses (a faint trail leads across the south side and intermittently joins with an old washed-out road). The boulders are also reached from the north side from campsite #8 or the Turkey Rock Access trail. Walk through the gap between Turkey Perch and Turkey Tail's north face.

Quivering Quill Blocks

These boulders sit in clear sight of the classic Quivering Quill 5.10d crack (faces north). Problems range from V0 slabs to small V2s.

V0-V2

Additional Turkey Perch Blocks

There is a huge boulderfield below the ultra-popular cracks on the south face of Turkey Perch. Problems range from V0 (with real bad landings) to V2 (with not-so-bad landings).

Bottom of the Heap Blocks

These boulders are the lowest boulders on the hillside below the south face of Turkey Perch. Scattered throughout the boulderfield are a handful of higher quality lines, with plenty of potential for new problems.

Blood Boulder

This is one of the lowest blocks in the boulderfield, with a view of an old tan trailer to the south. A roadbed is 60 yards to the south before the trailer. The problems are on the south face.

V0-V2

1. V0
Climb the left arete on the south face.

2. V6
Right of #1 in a left-facing dihedral with an atrocious finish. The rock is fragile at the lip.

Fun Gotti Boulder

Directly behind the Blood Boulder to the north five yards. To the north from Fun Gotti is a beautiful, thin, vertical face that spits off all attempts—well mine anyway.

1. V0 (not pictured)
Climb the north slab.

2. V2
Climb the overhanging south face to a knife-edge arete and finishing slab. A traverse can be done from the right.

***Note: The fires of 2002 may create closures in the Turkey Rock area for some time.

Phillip Benningfield on Tragedy Resides in You   photo: Jay Droeger

RED CLIFF

The bouldering at Red Cliff consists of a many developed areas (not all covered here), which, being shaded and at 9000 feet, escape the worst summer heat, but not all of it; the main area is described in *Colorado Bouldering*. The two areas highlighted here are not only good complements to the excellent main Kluttergarden, but all the areas have solid granite in the same vicinity: so a session could easily include all the developed areas.

Directions: Take US Route 24 south from Interstate 70 (exit #171). Follow the highway through Minturn and up past the bridge by Red Cliff. Drive to the south entrance for Red Cliff and park in the wide parking area on the right. Walk directly across the highway to a dirt road then head left. The easy hike takes a couple of minutes, max! When parking, DO NOT block the public bus stop! If the parking lot is nearly full please park further south down Highway 24 (in roadside pullouts or at the Hornsilver Day Use Area a half-mile south on the highway).

***Please tread ever-so-lightly when climbing at Red Cliff's dump.

THE KLUTTERGARDEN ETC.

This area has numerous tiny blocks with a handful of climbable boulders; the area is mostly devoid of the old machines found at The Kluttergarden. To reach The Kluttergarden Etc. boulders walk down the dirt road to the main Kluttergarden (you walk right through the middle of the boulderfield) then go approximately 175 yards further. The dirt road goes under the power line, and the boulders are roadside and to the northeast before heading downhill.

VO Block

VO BLOCK

This lone boulder sits off the road 25 yards and past an old fire pit. It has an overhanging arete on the south side (V3). All other problems on the boulder are V0 and make for uneventful warm-ups.

RED BOULDER

Uphill from the V0 Block to the east about 45 yards. This boulder and its neighbor are easily seen through the trees.

1. V0 ** 🪨🪨

A boulder problem requiring a mixture of stupidity and curiosity to climb. The landing defines Bad Landing but the climb is fun and worthwhile. The problem heads up the middle of the west face on good crimps to progressively better holds.

Red Boulder ⚠

2. V3 *
Climb the southwest arete on good sidepulls to a throw for the lip or hard crimping over an unsuitable landing.

3. V1
Climb the horribly sharp right side of the south face.

WHITE RIGHT BOULDER
The huge block adjacent to Red Boulder, with an undercut roof at seven feet, on the west face.

1. V0
Climb up the dirty left side of the north face.

2. V0 *
Climb up the open north face dihedral. A V3 starts on the sloping ramp left of the dihedral and finishes in the dihedral.

3. V1
Climb out the left side of the roof on the west face, starting from a big jug.

4. V3
Climb out the filthy right side of the west face roof. A difficult problem is immediately right, through the miniature overlaps.

5. V1
Climb—or don't if you are smart—the loose southwest arete.

Additional Blocks (pictured below)

This assortment of squatty boulders is located along the road before heading northeast to the better and bigger blocks. Problems range from V0 to V5 sit down starts.

V3

V3

SIGN BOULDER

A singular boulder graced with solid rock and distinctive problems. The boulder is visible from the parking area on Highway 24 to the east above the sign for Leadville and Buena Vista. Walk up the hillside on a trail, which starts off the dirt road, to reach the boulder.

**1. V2 ** **
Climb the vertical line on the left side of the west face. Easy up to the midway jug, then you encounter a sloping edge to reach the top.

**2. V2 * **
Just right of #1 up the right-diagonaling seam.

3. V1 🖐
Climb up the far right side of the south face in a broken ramp to a long reach at the top.

4. V6 ** 🖐
Climb up the southeast arete staying on the south face.

5. V5 * 🖐
Climb up the blunt south face arete right of the black stripes starting with a jump to reach the left-hand sidepull.

6. V3
Climb up the thin edges on the southeast face (left of the broken rock).

Colorado Bouldering sets the standard for bouldering guides in Colorado. If your looking for those classic Colorado areas, this is the book.

Colorado Bouldering 2 seeks the "off the beaten path" bouldering experience. This new edition highlights areas which have seen a boom in development since the first guide.

Get the Collection!

.

More Red Cliff in the original Colorado Bouldering

KLUTTERGARDEN ADDITIONS
UPDATES TO THE ORIGINAL COLORADO BOULDERING

The main and most developed area at Red Cliff. See Colorado Bouldering (page 237) for more information.

BOULDER F (SEE INTRO PHOTO TO RED CLIFF)

The largest block by the powerlines, with a tall southwest face undercut on the left side. Walk through the first set of boulders along the dirt road then look right across the meadow and Boulder F sits out in the open facing the road.

V3

On the far left side of the roof start standing and muckle over the lip. A direct start boosts the grade substantially.

Tragedy Resides in You V6 😊 🦶

A terrifying escapade—rather like dealing with pissy locals. Start on the right side of the undercut roof and dyno from crappy holds to gain the small right-facing corner. Be ever-so careful climbing the problem unless some fine person went to the trouble of cleaning the corner.

Anaphylactic Shock V6 * 😊

This problem begins in the low slot and moves up and left through indistinct holds. The problem begins the same as Sticky Fingers (see Colorado Bouldering, page 241).

BOULDER I

Continue north along the powerlines past two large blocks to a boulder within the woods (See Colorado Bouldering page 242). A steep west face has a small adjacent boulder lying under it with a plethora of sloping and micro holds that have been beaten into submission to create problems verging on V10—and maybe, just maybe V11. The problems are far too contrived to describe. Rest assured plenty of leathery flesh is necessary to pull on the horrifically minute crimps.

CHAPMAN / HAGERMAN

Krong on the Sunshine Boulder   photo: Chris Goplerud

CHAPMAN RESERVOIR

Chapman Reservoir area has a concentration of boulders near the water and sporadic blocks spread up the western side of Hagerman Pass. The granite boulders are very diverse. The boulder fields around Chapman Reservoir tend towards thin and lower quality, the Hagerman Pass boulders tend to be smooth as butter and crisp.

Directions: From Basalt drive east up Fryingpan Road (FR 105) towards Ruedi Reservoir (a couple of decent boulders are passed before reaching Ruedi). Pass the reservoir and continue past Meredith (an occasional granite block is roadside) for six miles. Turn right for Chapman Reservoir (dirt) and drive to the Group Site gate (may be closed) and park. Walk up the dirt road (east) to reach the boulders.

CANINE BOULDER

Two huge blocks, once one, have been split down the middle forming a wide chimney. The uphill block has a couple of extremely tall problems on the southeast face.

Directions: From the gate take the obvious trail on the right for 175 yards (southeast) up the hillside.

1. V3 🚗

Climb the tall middle section of the southeast face.

2. V0/V1 🚗

Climb the shorter right side of the boulder. Exit the boulder to the right.

BOULDER A NUMBER ONE

This block sits just off the right side of the dirt road after a short walk from the gate.

1. V3 *

Traverse the north face; many options to head upwards before reaching the west face.

2. V3 *

Climb the open scoop on the left side of the west face.

3. V5 *

Climb the southwest arete starting from the west face.

4. V0

Climb the south face slab.

(NOT PICTURED)

A set of boulders sits on the left side of the road a minute past Boulder A Number One. It is unknown whether any problems have been done on the block.

CAMPSITE 22 BOULDERS

A pair of boulders located up the road a short distance from Unknown Ascents. Look for a trail sign on the left and follow the trail leading to the right off the road for 80 yards to the boulders. The described boulders are only a taste of the boulders in the area as many more sit on the hillside to the west.

ROOF BOULDER

The first boulder encountered on the left side of the trail. A distinct head-height roof is on the east face.

1. V1

The overhang on the far left side of the east face in the chasm.

2. V5

Climb the left side of the roof on sharp holds. The problem starts off underclings to painful crimpers over the roof. Not a clean problem.

BACK BOULDER

This block rests on the southeast side of Roof Boulder and has a number of vertical problems on the south and east faces.

1. V1 *

Climb the east-face traverse from left to right.

2. V1 *

Climb directly up the vertical south face on positive edges.

3. V0

A one-move-wonder slab on the low-angle east face. Not visible on photo.

4. Trite Bologna V2 **

Probably the best problem in the Campsite 22 boulders. Climb the north face, starting in a left-facing corner, to slopers at the top. The problem is V4 from a sds.

Due West Boulder (not pictured)

This lone boulder sits directly across the trail and up the hill a short distance (easily seen from the trail) from the Campsite 22 Boulders.

1. V0
Climb the black south face. Not clean.

2. V3
Climb the southeast arete.

3. V0
Climb the low-angle east face.

Giant Steps Boulder

From the east face of the Back Boulder head east through a drainage for approximately 100 yards. The boulder sits on the edge of the Group Campsites.

Giant Steps V4 *
A difficult slab that climbs up the thin west face.

***More unrecorded problems have been done on the boulders located past the Group Campsites. To reach these boulders continue on the dirt road past the trail sign and enter the Group Campsite then continue east on the road to the boulders.

HAGERMAN PASS BOULDERS

These sporadic boulders are located on the west side of the pass past Chapman Reservoir area. There is one main block located up FR 105 past the intersection with FR 505.

Many more possibilities for first ascents, as well as problems previously done but unrecorded here, await the industrious boulderer further up the pass, or on the trudge up Ivanhoe Creek from the hairpin turn on FR 105. A 4x4 is necessary to reach the higher boulders on the pass.

SUNSHINE BOULDER

A spectacularly clean granite boulder with a magnificent view of the upper Fryingpan Valley and the Hunter Fryingpan Wilderness to the south. The boulder looks insignificant from the road (the short side faces the road).

Directions: From the hairpin turn (after driving east past Chapman Reservoir) drive one mile up FR 105 (headed northwest) to boulders on the left side of the road.

1. V5 **
A sds problem on the far left side of the boulder with a hard move to start.

2. V6 **
Just right of #1, start on good edges and move left and utilize the left-facing corner to better holds up high.

3. V8 **
Right of #2, climb the right-angling seam.

4. V?
A difficult traverse along the bottom of the boulder from right to left ending on #2 or continue to #1.

5. V6 **
Climb the blunt corner on the right side of the boulder before heading around the corner. A few variations exist to this problem.

6. V2 **
Climb up the only part of the boulder's south face with obvious good holds.

7. V4 *
Climb the thin southeast face. There a multitude of small edges so find the V4 sequence or tweak out on the thinner edges for a harder variation.

GREEN BOULDER (NOT PICTURED)
The slabby boulder east of the Sunshine Boulder. A couple of tall dirty slabs (V0) can be done on the southwest face.

Chris Goplerud on the Chick Climb   photo: Phillip Benningfield

INDEPENDENCE PASS

The Pass is graced with more kick-ass boulders than most alpine areas and easy access makes it perfect for the lazy boulderer. At a high elevation between 9000 and 10,000 feet the boulders stay near-dreamy throughout the summer and crisp and cold until the winter blankets the boulderfields with an impenetrable snow pack. Every year the industrious locals unearth new areas, and the past two years have been no exception. The boulders included here are only a small sampling of the fare.

Directions: The areas listed are all located in exact miles from the intersection of State Route 82 (Original Street) and Cooper Avenue on the east side of Aspen.

Black Caesar Boulder *is located on the left side of the road (basically in the roadway) at 9.1 miles (just after passing the roadside expanse of the Lower Grotto Wall and before Lincoln Creek Road). Park at the Grotto Wall parking area and walk up the road.*

James Brown Boulders *are located at 10.8 miles. Park in a righthand pullout and cross the highway. Follow a number of paths towards Wild Rock staying to the left side of the massive talus/boulderfield (approximately 100 yards northwest from the highway). The boulders are located on the flat terrain below the talus slope.*

Upper Boulderfield (Bulldog Boulders)
You can't miss these worthwhile boulders at 11.1 miles up the Pass on the left. A huge parking lot abuts the boulders.

BLACK CAESAR BOULDER

This cliffband is located at the thinnest section of pavement, for two cars, in the entire state. Three distinct problems can be done in the V3 to V6 range.

JAMES BROWN BOULDERS

A newly developed zone of four or so blocks that revolve around the neighborly James Brown Boulder (three massive blocks next to one another). There are plenty of high problems with questionable landings, but a few lines are plenty safe with a couple of pads.

FIRST BOULDER

A lone block 15 yards east before running smack dab into the James Brown Boulder.

1. V3 *
Climb the northeast overhanging arete starting on the left and moving to the right.

2. V2
The short low start variation to #1.

JAMES BROWN BOULDER

(problems listed left to right)
The boulder (15 yards west of First Boulder) sits closest to the talus slope headed up to Wild Rock and still on flat ground. A distinct boulder on the north side of the massive three-block collection.

1. It's a Man's World V5 **
The super tall gray east face. The epitome of a bad landing as the tall problem rests gingerly on a shelf. A fall up high could be rather catastrophic without many a pad and spotter.

2. Funky President V4 **
Climb the right side of the northeast arete. A problem of the same grade, maybe a tad harder, climbs the left side of the arete over a bad landing .

3. Hot Pants V3 **
Start on good edges on the north face. Gain the triangular hold then move right to finish.

Funky President

4. Sex Machine V4 *
Start on the small crimps directly below the triangular hold and climb straight up.

V3 * 🔵 🟢 (pictured right)

A lone problem uphill 20 yards to the north that faces southwest and climbs left of the arete. The backside of this huge boulder has a V4 on the far right side and left of the arete. Big-time projects are on the face left of the V4.

JB MIDDLE (NOT PICTURED)

The middle boulder of the three that constitute the James Brown Boulders.

1. V4

Climb the tall face up the black rock left of the tree.

2. Body Count V2 ** 🔵 🟢

Climb straight up the gray face. Located to the right of #1 and above the right-angling seam.

JB LEFT

The left boulder of the three, with a short overhanging tier capped by a sloping ramp and a vertical wall.

1. Moon Tide V1

Climb the left seam of the V seam to a glorious mantle topout.

2. Chick Climb V2 *

Climb the V seam on the low tier from a sds and finish up the right seam. A V2 climbs the up the arete to the right of #2.

3. American Hero V4 * 🔵

Climb up the golden white corner through a little contortionism. Be aware of a loose block up high.

MOUNTAIN BIKING
COLORADO'S
WESTERN SLOPE
THE VERY BEST RIDES FROM
ASPEN TO FRUITA

Climbing Rest Day?
Go Mountain Biking!

Explore the aspen groves on the Government Trail or take in the view of Capitol Peak on the Rim Trail. No matter which trail out of Mountain Biking Colorado's Western Slope you choose, the mountain biking around Aspen is amazing.

Pick up Phillip Benningfield's Mountain Biking Colorado's Western Slope ($9.95).

Rim Trail

Government Trail

UPPER BOULDERFIELD BOULDERS

Easily the most developed boulderfield on the Pass with over 40 problems. These newer additions are only a handful of the lines completed or waiting to be done.

LIGHTNING BOLT BOULDER AREA

The block is located 25 yards north of the parking area with a flat, white roof left of a crack. The boulder has four problems.

V3 * (not pictured)

A sds on a block just east of LB Boulder. The problem faces south and starts on a low overhang to a slab finish.

V4 * (not pictured)

A sds located directly behind (north) the Lightning Bolt Boulder. The problem is on a short overhang that faces down-valley. Muckle over onto the slab.

PAPPY BOULDER

This east-facing overhanging block is located uphill from the Loner (approximately 50-plus yards east of Lightning Bolt Boulder—a lone block trailside with a sds V4 on the north face) in the talus.

1. El Vere V6 *

Climb the far left side of the overhang.

2. Che It Loud V8 *

A low start up the middle of the overhang through a good undercling. Only V3 from the undercling to the top.

3. Pappy V1 *

The casual problem from the right side of the overhang climbing left along the lip.

Western Slope

GETTING AROUND THE CENTRAL MOUNTAINS

Colorado's Western Slope contains some of the state's best bouldering. If you are unfamiliar with the region a detailed map is recommended for travel to the various climbing areas. As mentioned elsewhere, this guidebook assumes a basic knowledge of the state and/or the resources to find small cities. The map below is provided for those who have forgotten their state map at home or are suffering from momentary geographic amnesia. It is assumed that the author's written descriptions in conjunction with this map will be adequate to locate the specific climbing areas.

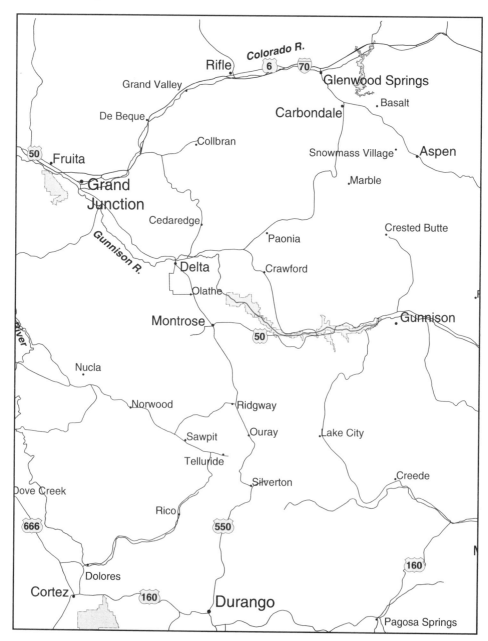

CRESTED BUTTE / GUNNISON

Sasha Halenda on Bernholtz Arete   photo: Phillip Benningfield

TAYLOR CANYON

The bouldering in Taylor seems somewhat limited considering the massive numbers of rocks and cliffs lining the road. What there is lends yet another opportunity to get cranking on solid granite at a higher elevation. The fishing ain't bad either.

Directions: From Almont (10.2 miles from Gunnison) head up FR 742 following signs for Taylor Reservoir for 7.5 miles. Park at the Sugar Cube (see Colorado Bouldering) at the entrance to North Fork Campground.

THE PILLAR

A distinct tall boulder found up the campground road 80-odd yards on the left. A tall slab side faces down-river and a steeper side up-river.

1. V4 ** 🚗
The slab that climbs the detached flake.

2. V7 * 🚗**
Easily the best-looking problem in Taylor Canyon! Climb the slightly overhanging face left of the wide crack to a good edge at mid-height then throw to a flat ledge.

THE GUTTER

Located down the road to the campground is an obvious cliff band on the left covered with chalk. The name of the cliff does not do it justice; it only provides an obvious name since a drainage pipe is found on the left side of the wall. The Gutter has 50 feet of solid granite and too many problems to list—a great place to get a pump. Problems range from V0 to V8 (harder as one moves right). A good sandbag V5 traverses the wall from left to right. A V3 slab

V3

is on the right of the wide chimney. Best not to top out—unless you like to solo on less-than-ideal rock.

BONZAI BOULDER

Either walk or park by campsite #8. From the campsite a trail leads along the river (may be washed out during spring runoff). Walk on this trail for about 10 minutes and the boulder will hit you in the face.

1. V0-V3 ** (not pictured)
A selection of problems on the north face from straight-ups to a traverse.

2. V2 **
Climb the northwest arete from a low start.

3. V6
Climb the ultra-thin seam right of #2 to sharp edges.

4. V0
The dirty west seam right of #3.

5. V1 **
Climb the west slab found before the left-angling arete of #6.

6. V4 *
Climb the southwest arete starting from thin edges on the south face then moving in to the sloping arete.

BONZAI EAST FACE PROBLEMS

7. Bonzai Straight Up V9 **
Start on lowest layback and slap up the blunt bulge on slopers and bad sidepulls.

8. Bonzai Left V6 **
Same start as #1, but move right then head straight up before the seam, leading to the tiny pine. Expect slopers and bad edges.

9. Bonzai Right V5 **
Same start as #1 then move right and climb up the seam, exiting on holds right on the tiny pine.

SKYLAND

What can be said? The granite at Skyland, an apt name for the boulderfield ling under the monolithic Mount Crested Butte, is undoubtedly the premier stone of the alpine zone. This fine, albeit limited, selection of additional boulders (*Colorado Bouldering* highlighted the main blocks) is itself worth a daylong trip.

Directions: New and improved! From Crested butte head south on US Route 135 to a left on FR 738 (Brush Creek Road) for the Skyland Country Club, then left at the clubhouse road and continue to the parking area for the Upper Loop Trail. Take a short walk uphill to a doubletrack then continue left on a singletrack to the main boulderfield. The new problems are located in the aspens to the northeast (see specific boulders for detailed directions).

HONE STONE

At the far north end of the main boulderfield along the Upper Loop Trail is a perfect block sitting on the left of the trail in an open meadow. Four problems of recent origin, or of newfound excitement have been added to the block with direct starts to the classic Bernholtz Arete (V6) and Tick Fever (V7).

V5
A problem left of Tick Fever and starting on the steep face then grovelling onto the slab.

Direct Tick Fever V9 *
The direct start to Tick Fever which climbs from a sit start up the middle of the south face. Use the thin left-angling edge to reach the starting holds on Tick Fever then do the Fever.

Direct Bernholtz Arete V8 * (see opener photo)
From a low start to the right of the stand-up holds on the arete climb into the regular route.

V5 * (pictured right)
The ultra-thin blunt northeast arete.

THE SHIELD

A massive orange and gold block to the northeast about 20 yards (across the Upper Loop Trail) from the hone Stone.

1. V2
Climb the left side of the huge burnt orange face.

2. V?
A big tall problem done by a big tall climber. Up the face right of #1.

ZACH'S CAMPGROUND

This collection of boulders has recently been developed and sports a couple of entertaining problems hidden away in the woods above the Upper Loop (closer to the Mt. Crested Butte cliffs).

Directions: The blocks are uphill and northeast from the Shield approximately 100 yards. A distinct trail can be taken from the Shield (20 yards northwest from of the Hone Stone) headed northwest then back northeast (look for faint game trails).

1. V5 *
The new line on the first boulder encountered from the faint trail. The problem begins in the open dihedral with a jump start to a good flat jug then hard moves to the finishing slab. A direct start will up the ante substantially.

2. V0
The easy left angling arête right of the open dihedral.

3. V6 *
Hard traverse on the back of the boulder from left to right.

4. V3 *
A sds on the blunt arête right of the traverse's end.

5. V5
Climb the left arête (to the far left of #1) using the right-hand face holds left of the low angle dihedral leading to the boulder's top.

6. V0
The low angle dihedral, which is one of the easiest ways to downclimb the block.

V3 *
Just left of the main block is a lone fin with a clean, slightly overhanging face starting from a low start. The arête to the left is an easy V0.

HARTMAN ROCKS

V3 on Highball Crack Area   photo: Phillip Benningfield

HARTMAN ROCKS

A few miles southwest from Gunnison is the best-smelling bouldering area in Colorado. The sagebrush expanse of intermittent granite outcrops has endless bouldering possibilities, and can satisfy the hungriest first ascentionist. Every year new areas are discovered and developed. Excellent side benefits of Hartman's are the superb views of the Elk Range, the San Juans and the Collegiates as well as terrific mountain biking. Pick up a map at Rock and Roll Sports that shows the trails, and locations of additional bouldering areas.

Directions:
From the intersection of US Route 50/135 take Hwy. 50 west towards Montrose for 1.6 miles to the brown sign for Hartman Rocks Recreation Area. Turn left on CR 38 (Gold Basin Road) and drive around the fence that borders the airport runway. Stay on this road for 2.4 miles—driving past a dirt factory.

For Super Model Area turn right at the sign for Hartman Rocks Recreation Area and go up the big hill (Heart Attack Hill). The second right past the cattle guard has a parking area in a cul-de-sac. For Bambie's Area continue on Gold Basin Road for 5.5 miles crossing over a cattle guard where the road turns to dirt. Park on the left just after the cattle guard. The Bambie Trail heads west directly after the cattle guard.

SUPER MODEL AREA

There are only a few problems at Hartman Rocks that are both beautiful and worth the flesh loss; The immaculate Super Model is one of them! The area around Super Model has a number of fine, short problems as well as others listed in Colorado Bouldering.

Directions:

Follow the directions on page 226. From the cul-de-sac walk down the hillside to the west and hit a dirt road. Go right down the steep road 100 yards veering left (a 4x4 truck can make this easily) around the rock formation and continue on the road past a sign (#4 on the right for a mountain bike trail). Look to the left for a cluster of pines and boulders (the beginning of the Super Model Area). Super Model is located west from the pines and small blocks (Groove Boulder) 30 yards.

SUPER MODEL BOULDER

A gorgeous north face with thin edges leading to a horizontal crack near the top. Tall slabs can be done on the west face at V0ish.

Super Model V5 ***

Climb the gold and tan face on very thin edges to an easy top-out.

WEST BLOCK

The westernmost boulder of the three.

1. Eric's Vicous Sloper Problem V4 *

The west block in the cluster, located a few feet from Groove Boulder. A sds matched on the left sloper then up to a sharp set of edges.

2. V0

On the west face is a casual slab.

NAMELESS BOULDER

The middle block of the three, with problems on the west face.

1. V1

A crappy little edge affair on the far left of the west face.

2. V3 *

Climb left from the right-angling crack up thin edges to a pebble at the top.

3. V2 *

The right problem starting from the crack then muckling on to sloping arete.

4. V0

A bad problem starting off the incut edge left of the tree to the jug at the top of the face.

GROOVE BOULDER

The easternmost block of the three.

1. V2 * (not pictured)

Climb the west face up good sharp edges.

2. V3 **

From the black pebbles on the left side of the southeast face slap up the groove and exit straight up.

3. The Groove V1 *

When you figure out how to climb the groove, the problem is easy. Starts with the right hand on the dike and the left on the sloping black pebble.

BAMBIE'S BOULDERS

As with any area at Hartman Rocks there are boulders and cliff-bases littered with problems (many unrecorded due to sub-par rock). Bambie's Boulders certainly vies as one of the better areas to climb at, with its easy approach, decent quality, and a wide variety of problems to get all the juices flowing.

Directions: Hike up the Bambie Trail (a singletrack trail) following a barbed wire fence on the right and continue through a small aspen grove then past short pinnacles on the trail's right side. Right after the pinnacles pass a small block on the trail's left side. Walk 25 yards and look up the hillside on the right for the Hard Mantle Boulder (total distance from the road is 250 yards). To reach the main Bambie's Boulders area, walk west past the Hard Mantle Boulder up a very faint trail over slabs to the upper tier of rock (125 yards). To reach Whatever Dom Wants continue past Hard Mantle on the Bambie Trail for 80 yards (past a cliff band with a low roof above white rock) to a boulder on the right of the trail with "Lilly" scraped on the face. Take the drainage 30 yards past "Lilly" to the west and uphill approximately 50 yards to a west-facing boulder (Whatever Dom Wants).

HARD MANTLE BOULDER (NOT PICTURED)

A block 20 yards off the trail's right (west) with a distinct crack through a roof on the east face. Problems have not been done on the northwest face.

Hard Mantle V5 *

Climb the face below the crack and top out using the crack. A burly affair turning the lip.

LOOK MA BOULDER

A distinctive lichen-covered block that has a large east-facing visor hanging out from the upper tier of rock. Approximately 125 yards west above Hard Mantle Boulder.

1. Look Ma V2 *** 🚗 🖐 (pictured at right)
No kidding! The fall from up high on Look Ma could be catastrophic. Climb the southwest face above a jumble of rock on small edges to the horn on the right blunt arete then the top.

2. Don't Look Ma V3 🖐
On the northeast face is a harder problem above yet more jumbled rock.

THE WORM AREA
Located on the same tier as Look Ma Boulder and 20 yards to the north.

1. The Worm V0 🚗 🖐
This 30-plus-foot problem is located just uphill 20 yards from Look Ma Boulder and faces Look Ma Boulder. A good warm-up, facing southeast, on questionable rock.

2. V0 *
The left problem that climbs into excellent patina rock. Downclimb the gully between this problem and The Worm.

3. V0
The crack to the face and patina rock. Continuing up the crack is also V0. Same downclimb as #2.

****Located just to the southwest from Look Ma in a lower tier is a short block with a problem up the left side and a traverse.

1. V2 *
Climb from a sds up the left side to sharp edges and slopers.

2. V5
Traverse the lip of the boulder either way for a painful and difficult outing.

The next four problems are located to the southeast from The Worm, 15 yards along a set of separate boulders leading to the east. More lines can be done to the north on numerous small blocks.

1. V2 *
Climb the left arete to small edges on the face and an easy slab finish.

2. V3 **
Climb the right side of the block from a left-hand sidepull and right-hand edge to the slab finish.

3. V2 *
The tall face found directly right and above the previous two problems on a tall block in a passageway. Climb the left side of the extremely tall face.

4. V2
The right exit up the tall face avoiding the friable flake up high.

5. V3 *
Directly above the tall face is a slightly overhanging boulder with a left-leaning seam.

V2 * (pictured at right)
The west-facing crack found west of The Worm and around the corner. Very tall, and dirty on the exit. A V1 climbs right of the crack.

HIGHBALL CRACK WALL
The next six problems are on the lowest tier, about 20 yards west from The Worm. Walk past the west-facing V2 crack and down to the west to a set of tall cracks, facing northwest, above a short slab. The lichen on the wall is very colorful. Any fall from high on the cracks would most likely result in a shattered something, perhaps a pelvis.

1. V0 *
You will break your leg if you pitch off this dihedral on the left side of the crag.

2. V3
Climb the face just right of the dihedral. The first ascentionist stated these words 15 feet up the problem: "Don't break!

Don't break! Keep going!" The problem looks magnificent but needs a cleaning.

3. V1 *

The first left-leaning crack right from the dihedral. The lower slab still juts out on this problem.

4. V1 *

Just to the right is an easier crack problem.

5. V5 *

From a low start off a big sloper (just right of a mound of bat guano) dyno up to a right-facing corner then continue up.

6. V0

The dirty crack right of the V5.

Whatever Dom Wants V5 *

J. Houck on Whatever Dom Wants
photo: Droeger

If you knew who Dominique was you'd be submissive too. Climb the southwest face up secure sidepulls to a horrifying belly-scraping top-out on slopers. See the introduction for directions.

LILLY BOULDERS (NOT PICTURED)

Just 20 yards west off the Bambie Trail (80 yards past the turn at the Hard Mantle Boulder) is a boulder with "Lilly" scraped on it. Two blocks sit on opposite sides of Lilly with problems on them.

V4 *

On the south boulder adjacent to Lilly is a problem on the west face. Start from a flat jug then around to an edge on the north face then the top.

V5 *

Climb the overhanging south arete 15 feet north of Lilly.

V0 *

This problem truly has a bad landing! Climbs the south-facing dike 30 feet above and west of Lilly.

Ned Harris experiences a Perfect 10 on Heart Boulder

MONTE VISTA'S BOULDER CITY

The expanse of rhyolite boulders near Monte Vista is an impressive sight. Every size and shape of burnt orange and terracotta hued boulder can be found, with all kinds of huecos, pockets and edges. The quality of the bouldering does not always match the appearance, because the texture and fragility of the rock can be detrimental to flesh and psyche. Many of the boulders are house-sized, but short safe problems exist; the landings tend towards flat, which is little relief on some of the 25-foot tall journeys. If you are a spoiled brat (i.e. hate pain and blood) when it comes to bouldering, then avoid Monte Vista, but hardpersons will lap it up.

*** the problems described here are not the full extent of new lines ...

Directions: From Monte Vista take CO 15 south from the intersection of CO 15/US 160 for 12.2 miles. The road turns to dirt at the intersection of CO 15/FR 250. Take a right (headed west) and drive 8.3 miles passing through a small rhyolite canyon and past a National Forest sign. Go left on FR 2502A (the sign may not be present); FR 2502A is the second dirt road on the left after passing through the rhyolite canyon. Drive 0.5 mile to the boulders on the left of the road.

HEART BOULDER

This is the house-sized boulder first encountered down FR 2502A, with numerous large huecos big enough to sit in or squat under. The "heart" is evident when looking at the north face. Problems on this boulder tend toward big and bad-ass. Bring as many crash pads as you can muster.

1. V4 ***

From a low start on the southeast face, climb out of the white hueco then up the pocketed face to a casual top-out.

2. Rebekah V5 *** 🚗

Climb up and up and up the black stripe on the north face starting right of the undercut roof. Exit above the low roof on good edges to a bomber pocket. A direct start (V7) to this problem starts under the roof on the small huecos and traverses onto the face.

3. Perfect 10 V3 *** 🚗

Just right of #2, before the steepest part of the north face, climb up, up and away on the pocketed wall. Many small edges can be used between the more obvious pockets to create ten excellent moves.

4. Man in the Moon V3 *** 🚗

Again start right in the steeper black rock and climb straight up the sharp edges and pockets. This line is perfectly spectacular—just like its neighbors.

FIRESIDE BOULDER

The smoke-stained boulder with a big firepit next to it, 10 yards north of Heart Boulder.

1. V0

The line left of the overhang and firepit.

2. V1 *

The line on the right of the overhang. Start off the hueco and go to good pockets.

3. V3 *

On the back is a colorful clean-pocketed face ending on a left-leaning arete.

Scoop Boulder (not pictured)

Uphill to the north 50 yards from Heart Boulder. The south-facing scoop is easily visible from Heart Boulder.

1. V3 *
On the right edge of the scoop, climb up the rough pockets to a big dirty slab.

East Scoop Block (not pictured)

This massive boulder is located five yards east of the Scoop Boulder. The west face is an unmowed lawn of lichen. The east face offers clean lines with bad landings. The easiest downclimb is on the north face.

1. V2 **
Climb the left side of the southeast face on pockets.

2. V0 *
The slab line left of the cleanest face and right of #1.

3. V3 **
Climb the clean face under the small roof on excellent pockets then pull over on small holds to a scary exit.

Substantial Slab Boulder

Directly above Scoop Boulder to the north 15 yards. A nice flat area, and a massive fir tree, is at the base of the problems.

1. V?
Climb the west face on pockets.

2. V?
The left, blunt, southwest arete. A hard start to gain the sinker two-finger pocket.

3. V0 **
The clean south slab left of the seam.

4. V0 *
Climb the left-angling seam. The top is dirty—so climb under control.

5. The Slab V0 **
Just to the right of the huge fir is a 25-foot slab starting before the wall gets steeper.

6. V?
Pull through the steep lower wall to the monster slab above.

7. V?
Climb the extremely tall vertical southeast face.

BLACK BLOCK

Located 20 yards east of the Heart Boulder.
The best problems reside on the east face.
Many other problems exist beyond those
listed.

1. V2 **
The left side of the east face, before the
arete. Perfect landing.

2. V1 **
Climb up just right of #1 on good edges. Perfect landing.

3. V? **
A hard problem starting just left of the low hueco and making two hard moves at the start. A
low start boosts the grade to V?+.

4.V2 *
Climb the left side of the scoop facing the dirt road. Excellent pockets to a friable exit.

WARM-UP SLAB

A low-angle boulder located 30 yards east of the
Black Block. All problems on the west face are V0.

V1 *
Directly behind the Warm-up Slab is a small
block with two V1 problems.

DIAGONAL SEAM BLOCK (NOT PICTURED)

A big boulder located 80 yards uphill from the
Warm-up Slab. A distinct diagonal seam splits the brown west face.

V0s on Warm-up Slab

1. V3 **
A great warm-up traverse from right to left along the seam and exiting before the north face.

2. V2
The left line before the wall overhangs the adjacent boulder. Long descent across a dirty slab.

3. V0
The problem just right of #2. Same award-winning slab descent.

PETRA BLOCK

This mixed-quality block is located 40 yards east of the Warm-up Slab. A gorgeous lichen-covered arete faces northwest with a wide wall stretching to the south face.

1. Allesandrina V1 ** (pictured at right)

Climb the beautiful northwest arete, starting off the block. A low start adds quite a punch to the festivities.

2. V5 **

Just right of #1 is a pocketed face to a hard move to reach the lip.

3. Petra V4 **

Climb the black south face on positive edges and a great pocket.

4. V3

The scooped face to the right of Petra.

ROAD BLOCK (NOT PICTURED)

The boulder sitting directly below the Petra Block a mere 10 yards. The pocketed west face (facing the road) has problems.

1. V6 *

Climb the gold face straight up at the left end of the diagonal seam.

2. V4 *

Starts right of #1 then heads straight up and left of obvious loose flake.

THE HUECO AREA

Another vast expanse of good blocks located 0.3 miles down FR 2502A from Heart Boulder or a short three-minute walk. The blocks are just off the road on the left.

THE ROOT CANAL

A distinctive boulder with a small tunnel through the entire base (the boulder looks like a tooth). The block sits 25 feet from the dirt road and has problems up every side. The downclimb, which faces the road, is a chore at V0 and loose and licheny.

1. Triage V2 ** (pictured at right)

On the west face is a pocketed problem with one painful lock-off.

2. The Nasty Downclimb V0
The only way off the boulder besides pitching 12 feet onto pads. A loose flake defines the start and end.

3. V1 *
The slab affair to the right of #2 and before the silken tan and red face.

4. V7 **
Climb the thin pocketed face left of the southeast arete.

5. V6 *
Climb straight up the east face on pockets and the area's sharpest edges. The top-out has massive jugs.

6. V?
The east arete on small pockets.

7. Lolita V4 **
Climb up the middle of the north face to an obvious edge and pocket then move right to bad edges and an insecure top-out.

8. V4 *
The harder V4 line starting from the bomber pocket on the northwest corner and exiting up the same minute edges as Lolita.

V1 * (pictured right)
Directly across the road from Root Canal is a maroon face, with a big pocket at mid-height, facing the road. A hueco problem (V2) sits just to the left on an adjacent boulder and is much harder from a sds.

V1

V1 *
On the boulder just south from Root Canal is a short problem out the hueco off a bomber edge and tiny pocket. One move to the top flop-out moves.

Kia V4 ** (pictured right)
Found on the northwest arete 20 yards to the north from Root Canal (on the way to the Hueco Boulder). Start low on the sloping hueco with tiny pockets then move up over the lip to the right slab face.

Kia

Brown Eye V2 ** (pictured top left)
Found 25 yards west of Root Canal. Climb the west face's eye.

Finger Thumb V3 * (pictured top right)
Found 20 yards west of Brown Eye. Climb the south seam. A V1 climbs the dirty southeast slab to the right.

THE HUECO BOULDER
From Root Canal walk uphill to the north 40 yards past Kia and a slabby boulder (many V0s can be done, with a nice flat top to hang out on). The problems on the Hueco Boulder face southwest and begin in a huge overhang.

1. White Guilt V4 ** (pictured up and left)
The left hueco on the steep southwest face. A hard start, off the hueco's left side, to a huge ledge.

2. Monika V6 * (pictured up and right)**
Start with the right hand in the white hueco and the left hand in the lowest undercling. Move up and over the lip to the big pockets and a harrowing slab finish. The Bathtub direct start is V9 and begins as low as possible in the inverted bathtub.

V0s (pictured right)
Fifteen yards to the northwest is a slew of low-angle V0 slab problems on two blocks that are easily visible from Hueco Boulder.

Yasmine's Boulder

Just up the hill to the north from Hueco Boulder is an obvious overhanging arete.

1. Cliché V4 **

Climb the golden face left of #2, utilizing the bomber edges and some questionable laybacks.

2. Yasmine's Arete V5 ***

A near-perfect arete, except for the pain in the tips. Starts low on the arete to good pockets then a scary throw and top out.

3. V0s

The excellent pocketed slabs around the corner on the north face.

4. V0 to V3

More problems exist on the south side—but the rock hurts soooo bad!

5. DYC V3 ** (not pictured)

The north-facing hueco left of Cliché. Starts low on the lovely bat dung.

The Reverend

Yet another big boulder sitting up the hillside from Root Canal. Walk to the north 100 yards past a couple of enormous blocks. The problems reside on the northeast face and rarely see the light of day. The downclimbs require patience and/or a little endurance to downclimb #1.

1. Created by God V0 *

Climb the left side of the face starting on pockets or a sharp edge to the biggest jugs in the area. Finish up the cruiser edges to the top. This is the easiest downclimb.

2. Loved by All V3 *

Climb up the middle of the face starting on a good pinch then into the right-facing mini-corner and the top pockets and edges.

3. Feared by Satan V5 **

Start the same as #2 then move right to a good layback and bomber jug. The straight-up exit slab is a serious affair (no holds visible to the naked eye) but fortunately the line exits immediately right of the exit for #2.

THE HONEYCOMB V1 *
Down the gully to the left (east) of The Reverend approximately 25 yards. The problem climbs through—you guessed it—a honeycombed face.

HUECO WARM-UPS
Head uphill and to the right 70 yards from Root Canal (a little right of the enormous blocks separating Root Canal and The Reverend). The wall is littered with numerous huecos and the problems face the dirt road. Every line on this wall is a blast!

1. V3 **
The left problem. It slaps over the lip from a good two-finger pocket.

2. V2 **
Climb the problem just right of #1.

3. V2 **
Start in the right side of the larger huecos to monodoigts and a balancy top-out.

4. V3 **
The rightmost pocketed face in the small corridor.

LESS THAN DESIRABLE BOULDER
Directly down the hill from Hueco Warm-up wall and 40 yards east from Root Canal is a large rectangular block.

1. V2 **
Climb the thin southeast arete.

2. V0
A couple of dirty V0 problems climb the southwest face.

NED'S WONDERLAND OF ROCK

Another 40 yards east from Less than Desirable are two blocks with extremely nice problems on short north-facing overhangs. The boulders are a few yards from the dirt road.

UPPER NED

The block further from the road than Lower Ned.

1. V4 **

A low start on the north face and left of the corner. Climbs to a shallow pocket and bad edge then to the top. A dynamic problem is just right.

2. V3 **

A low start on the northwest face, then up good edges and pockets.

LOWER NED

The block closer to the dirt road.

1. V4 **

Another low start on the north face, up through great edges then pockets.

2. V4 **

Just right, start low to a throw to the ramp and a long reach over the top.

3. V4 **

Start off the ramp and move right to the left-facing mini-ramp with a pocket and exit.

4. V3 *

Climb the west arete.

5. V0

Climb the southwest face left side up the slab.

NED'S POCKET WALL (NOT PICTURED)

Yet another big boulder that looks like all the others. Walk east approximately 60 yards (do not go uphill) staying in the open meadow (go up before reaching a large boulder with dirty seams and possible chalk). Then walk straight uphill 20 yards—the V3 pocketed face faces uphill.

1. V0 🌀

Climb the dirty east face.

2. V3 **

Climb the short, pocketed northeast face. If you like shallow two-finger pockets you'll dig this.

GOLDEN FACE BLOCK

A perfect golden west face with an impressive left-trending arch. Walk 60 yards east across the hillside (do not go up) from Ned's Pocket Wall.

1. V3 **

Climb the seam on the left side of the west face.

THE ELDO CONTINGENT'S AREA

Fifty yards straight uphill from the Golden Face is an alcove with three sides. An extremely tall left wall is undercut at the base with a wide chimney separating it from a gorgeous arete. A shorter clean face is right of the arete.

1. Eric's Arete V5 **

Climb the huge arete right of the wide chimney.

2. V0 to V3 *

On the shorter block right of #1 is a selection of problems moving around the corner.

UNAWEEP CANYON

Eric Candee climbing yet another nameless boulder   photo: Phillip Benningfield

UNAWEEP CANYON

This is a vast canyon littered with thousands of Dakota sandstone blocks. Unfortunately, it seems that for every ten blocks, only about one or two hold good enough rock for bouldering; however, these good ones are often excellent, with really fun problems. The boulders listed here cover the gamut of quality with the Upper Boulderfield and Grand Valley Overlook holding the best problems. Rest assured there are hundreds of unrecorded and undone problems in the canyon. If you like some adventure in a bouldering session (explosive holds and slick lichen), Unaweep suffices. A great winter destination!

Directions:
From Grand Junction take US Route 50 south to Whitewater. Turn right on State Route 141 and drive a mile to enter the canyon. Areas are listed in mileage from the intersection of US 50 and State Route 141.

Texas Boulders/Cancel Christmas
This area is located 3.3 miles up the canyon on the right (just after the cattle guard). Take a right-hand dirt road to parking on either side of creek.
Texas Boulders are found by walking north above the dirt road from the parking (on the west side of the creek) for approximately 150 yards. The blocks are directly above the cattle guard on highway 141.
Cancel Christmas is found by walking along the dirt road southwest for a few minutes (stay on right-hand road). Approximately 100 yards past an old wooden drainage in the dirt road, head uphill to the west 80 yards. The boulders are found on the south end of a large meadow.

B.C.'s Western Boulders
These are located at the righthand pullout at 5.0 miles (Bone Park Area, with Fossil Boulder). A good place to camp. Additional directions included with boulders' descriptions.

Grand Valley Overlook Boulders
This collection of blocks is located 8.1 miles up SR 141 on the right. A large pullout is obvious with a sign for Grand Valley Overlook. The boulders are visible to the west across the creek from the pullout. Walk on a trail across the creek then take the dirt road 150 yards to the west.

Liquorstore Boulder
Same directions as Grand Valley but turn on to the left-hand dirt road at the beginning of the GV pullout. Park immediately then walk straight uphill 75 yards to a distinct traverse boulder.

TEXAS BOULDERS

Named for a large boulder shaped like Texas, with a toprope anchor for a southwest-facing crack problem. Some boulders in the vicinity have anchors but can be bouldered with a couple of pads.

ANCHOR BOULDER

A large block with excellent warm-ups on the south face. Toproping anchors are present. The downclimb is on the east face.

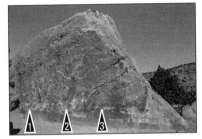

**1. V0 ** 🚐
The left problem on the south face. Good holds abound.

**2. V1 ** 🚐
The middle line up the tallest part of the face.

**3. V0 * 🚐
The right line on the south face.

HORIZONTAL CRACK BOULDER

A gritty block found 25 yards west of Anchor Boulder.

1. V?
The left line on the east face.

**2. V3 * 🕐
The right line. Start on good pockets to a sloping right-hand edge then to the top.

CORRIDOR BLOCK

A tall boulder found 39 yards to the north through a corridor from Anchor Boulder. Problems are on the northwest face. The downclimb is in the corridor.

**1. V3 ** 🚐
The arete dividing the north and west faces.

**2. V3 ** 🚐 👊
Climb the west face with an initial long reach. The higher holds are a little questionable.

**3. V0 🚐 👊
Climb the crack right of #2.

Cancel Christmas Block

A huge block with problems on the west and east faces. The boulder just northeast has a couple of V0s.

East Face

1. V3 *
The left set of pockets to the lip.

2. V4 *
Climb the middle of the face from good pockets then right hand up to another pocket then the top.

3. V3 *
The right line starting off a good pocket to the high pocket on #2.

West Face

1. Cancel Christmas V6 *
A committing line starting just right of the small boulder at the base. Excellent pockets lead to a difficult reach to gain the top.

2. The Grinch V3
A low start adjacent to the boulder on the right of the west face. The holds are questionable.

B.C.'s WESTERN BOULDERS

This area is easy to find by following a superb trail marked with cairns every 10-20 yards (don't expect all the cairns to be in place due to heavy bovine traffic). A collection of blocks found on the west side of the creek from the Fossil Boulder (the obvious block standing a stone's throw from Highway 141 with bone fossils on its east face). From Fossil Boulder walk southwest to a trail marked with cairns (follows a drainage to the creek). Cross the creek then uphill to a cow-trail intersection and go left approximately 100 yards to Artifact Boulder. Big Black Boulder and the Upper Boulderfield are found by continuing west on the marked (cairn) trail. Big Black is approx. 200 yards west and the Upper Boulderfield is 75 yards below the cliffs and on the west side of a dirt road.

ARTIFACT BOULDER

Somewhat of a novelty for Unaweep since the boulder has a near-horizontal roof on its south face. Problems on this block vary substantially in quality, and cows, and their detritus seem attracted to it like moths to a flame.

South face problems range from V1 to a V6 traverse. Detailed descriptions are left out; you'll know why when you walk by the boulder.

BIG BLACK

A beautiful lone block with decent quality problems along the north face (many contrived lines can be done). Problems on the east face are tall and V0.

North Face problems are listed from left to right.

1. V0 *** 🌦

An excellent line on the left arete. One of the better lines in the canyon.

2. V2 ** 🌦 ✊

Just right of #1 is a super-long reach from the starting holds to incut holds.

3. V3 * (not pictured)

From thin edges left of the crack climb straight up on ever-thinning edges.

4. V0 * (not pictured)

The crack on the right side of the block.

Upper Boulderfield

A collection of beautiful blocks sporting maroon and black stripes. This area is undoubtedly one of the funner in the entire canyon with ten or so climbable blocks nestled in the same zone. Problems listed range from incredibly tall V0 slabs to short V6s; many more nearby lines can be found and done.

Slabular Block

This is the first big boulder encountered, with a great south-facing warm-up slab. A comfortable flat rock sits adjacent to take the mandatory naps and get refreshments.

1. V0 *

The left side of the south face, up big holds.

2. V0 **

Climb the broken seam up the middle of the south face.

3. V1 *

Directly right of the seam, climb the not-so-obvious holds to the top.

4. V2 *

The blunt right arete, before the flat boulder. A hard start then it eases up.

5. V3 *

Sitting on the flat block climb up the sloping holds.

6. V1 *

Climb the face just to the right of #5.

West Boulders

Two blocks that sit just to the west of the Slabular Block.

First West Boulder

1. V2 **

Climb the northeast slab, and hope for the best when you reach out left. A safer exit can be done to the right.

2. West Crack V0

The short crack facing the Second West Boulder.

3. V0

Climb the west arete and don't fall!

SECOND WEST BOULDER

A shorter version of First West Boulder.
The north side has numerous sit-starts.

1. V2 **
The leftmost problem on the north face. A
sds makes it V4.

2. V6 *
A sds just left from the offset seam and #3.
One big move to get the ass off the dirt.

3. V4 *
A low start in the offset crack. It's V0 from a stand up start.

4. V0 *
The south face has a couple of nice V0 affairs.

SOUTHERN BLOCK (NOT PICTURED)

A lone boulder south from Slabular Block a mere 40 yards.

1. Let The Chips Fall Where They May V0
Climb the fragile east face.

2. V2 *
Climb the left-leaning sloping ramp to a dirty top-out. V4 from a low start.

EASTERN BLOCKS

A couple of lone problems can be found to the east of Slabular Block 25 to 40 yards away.

1. V3 **
The jump start problem of the
area. The first move can rebut
the easily swayed, but this is a
problem well worth a couple of
failed jumps.

2. V2s
There are a couple of reasonable problems on the easternmost boulder before the open
field area. One is vertical in a
corridor. The other faces the
field and starts steep to an easy
top-out.

GRAND VALLEY OVERLOOK AREA

Whether or not these boulders are newly developed does not matter; these are easily some of the best problems Unaweep has to offer. The rock is pretty good and the lines have very aesthetic movements. Besides, the boulders are so damn easy to find all your mental energy can be used to figure out sequences.

CHINESE ALGEBRA BOULDER

The name says it all. Found next to the dirt road.

1. V1 *
Climb the left side of the northeast face starting from a low fin and edge.

2. V2 **
Climb the line just right of #1 from a right-hand undercling and thin left edge. Then climb straight up to progressively better edges.

3. V2 🖐
Climb the right side of the northeast face eight feet left from the arete. The holds on this one are less than desirable.

4. Chinese Algebra V6 ***
Low start on the left side of the west face, then to bad slopers leading out to the right. A tough mantle problem exits after reaching the sloping lip.

5. V3 **
The right line out the overhang on the west face.

6. V1 *
Climb the brown rock on the far left side of the south face. A traverse can be done into this problem from the right.

7. V1 *
Climb the thin edges right of the juniper from a low start.

8. V0 *
Climb the arete just right of #7.

S CRACK BLOCK

A tall boulder found 40 yards to the north from Algebra. The south face is clean and burnt-orange.

1. V1 *
Climb the traverse on the northeast face then top out. Bad feet at the end of the traverse.

2. V0
Across the south face are many casual tall V0 slabs.

3. V2 *
Climb the southeast arete, with a long reach to gain the high finishing holds.

4. S Crack V1 *
Climb the crack on the southeast face.

5. S Seam V3 **
The right crack on the east face.

6. V?
The dirty, fragile righthand problem before the tree.

BOXCAR BOULDER
Found 30 yards uphill to the north from Algebra. The gorgeous southeast face is undercut on the left side.

1. V?
Start at overhang on the left side of the southeast face and pull onto face then up.

2. V4 *
Starts off ledge on the left before the undercut roof.

3. V3 *
Climb the middle seam on the southeast face with a boulder to land on.

4. V4 *
The ultra-thin seam right of #3 that peters out then opens up at a mono.

5. V0
Climb the right arete on the southeast face.

6. Racing the Sun V2 **
Climb the left side of the north face from a triangular hold to bad sloping edges.

A few shorter boulders are located 20 yards below the Boxcar. Problems range from V2 to V5.

ARETE BOULDER

This distinct block has two fine aretes surrounding the southeast face. It is located 40 yards uphill and west from the Boxcar Boulder.

1. V3 *

The left arete on the southeast face.

2. V4 ***

One of the classic problems in Unaweep Canyon! If you make only one trip definitely do this line. Start off the hueco then move left to a sidepull and a big throw. The top holds should be climbed on lightly.

3. Invisible Sun V6 **

Climb the right-angling seam on positive but minute edges, starting from the good edges with the foot thrown onto the big ledge.

4. V3 **

Climb the left arete on the southeast face.

5. V0

On the east face are a couple of V0 lines.

PINK FLOYD BOULDER

From Arete Boulder head northwest 100 yards across an open meadow towards the cliff bands. The boulder faces south and is as obvious as your nose.

1. V3

On the far left side of the south face is a seam that slabs out after the first moves.

2. Earthbound Misfit V3 ***

On the south face is a superb distinct problem, with a party trick start, to a pocket then outstanding pulls to the top. A brand-new V7 is just to the right.

3. Comfortably Numb V6 **

The hard line right of #2 in the black rock. Start low on crimps then pull to a sharp finger lock, then up. Watch out for the fragile lip holds!

4. V0

On the east face are a couple of uneventful V0 problems.

LIQUORSTORE BOULDER

A tall block located 75 yards towards the cliffband from the dirt road: directly across the road from the downhill start of the Grand Valley Overlook pullout.

1. V6 **

A long traverse from left to right along the north face. The top out is a little dicey.

2. Latina Heat V5 *

Up the left side of the north face starting from the decent flat holds along the traverse to a bad right-hand sloper then good pockets. Ends on the same holds as #3. An easier V1 is to the left.

3. V3 *

The problem just right of Latina Heat. Climb straight up.

4. V3 *

An arete problem is on the boulder adjacent (right) of Liquorstore.

Chris Goplerud freezing despite his proximity to some Latin Heat

ACCESS: It's every climber's concern

The Access Fund, a national, nonprofit climbers organization, works to keep climbing areas open and to conserve the climbing environment. Need help with closures? land acquisition? legal or land management issues? funding for trails and other projects? starting a local climbers' group? CALL US!

Climbers can help preserve access by being committed to leaving the environment in its natural state.

• **ASPIRE TO CLIMB WITHOUT LEAVING A TRACE** especially in environmentally sensitive areas like caves. Chalk can be a significant impact – don't use it around historic rock art. Pick up litter, and leave trees and plants intact.
• **DISPOSE OF HUMAN WASTE PROPERLY** Use toilets whenever possible. If toilets are not available, dig a "cat hole" at least six inches deep and 200 feet from any water, trails, campsites, or the base of climbs. Always pack out toilet paper. On big wall routes, use a "poop tube."
• **USE EXISTING TRAILS** Cutting switchbacks causes erosion. When walking off-trail, tread lightly, especially in the desert on cryptogamic soils. "Rim ecologies" (the clifftop) are often highly sensitive to disturbance.
• **BE DISCRETE WITH FIXED ANCHORS** Bolts are controversial and are not a convenience – don't place 'em unless they are really necessary. Camouflage all anchors. Remove unsightly slings from rappel stations.
• **RESPECT THE RULES** and speak up when other climbers don't. Expect restrictions in designated wilderness areas, rock art sites, caves, and to protect wildlife, especially nesting birds of prey. Power drills are illegal in wilderness and all national parks.
• **PARK AND CAMP IN DESIGNATED AREAS** Some climbing areas require a permit for overnight camping.
• **MAINTAIN A LOW PROFILE** Leave the boom box and day-glow clothing at home.
• **RESPECT PRIVATE PROPERTY** Be courteous to land owners. Don't climb where you're not wanted.
• **JOIN THE ACCESS FUND** To become a member, make a tax-deductible donation of $25.

your climbing future

The Access Fund
Your Climbing Future
PO Box 17010
Boulder, CO 80308
303.545.6772
www.accessfund.org

INDEX

Index

NOTES

NOTES

NOTES